Oxford International Primary

Maths
Practice Book

6

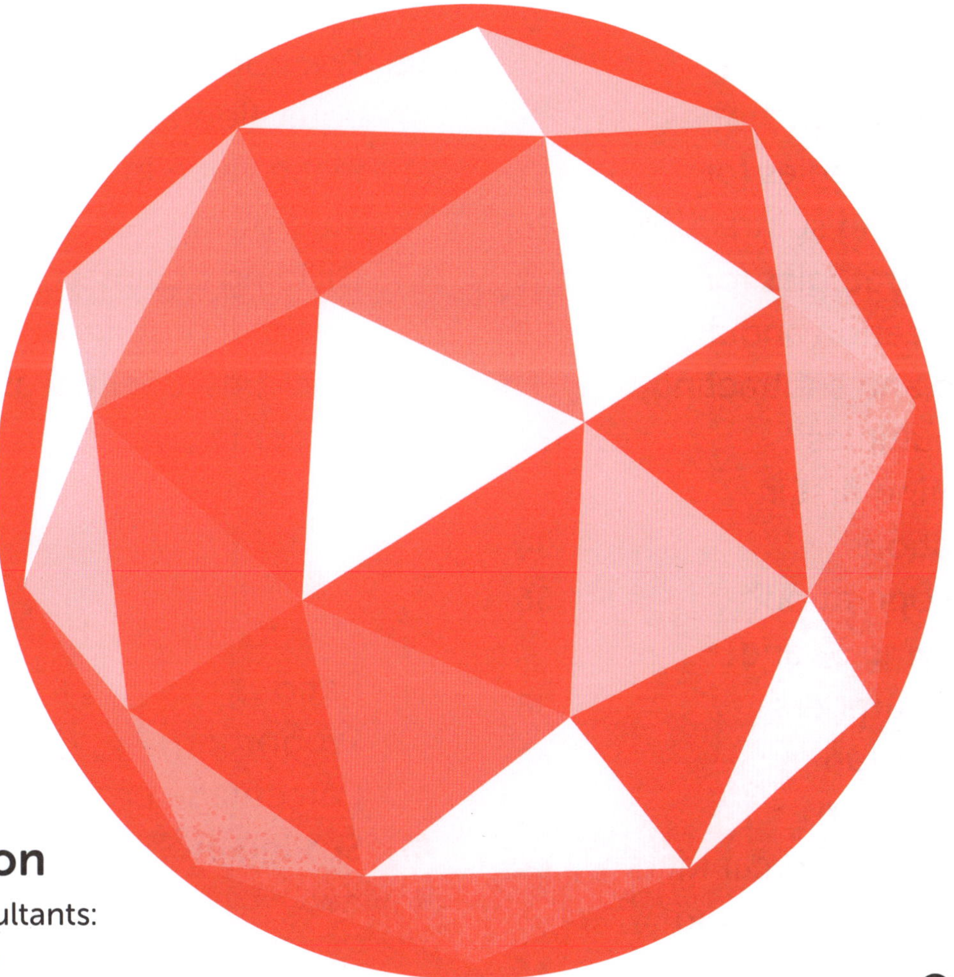

Tony Cotton

Language consultants:
John McMahon
Liz McMahon

OXFORD

Contents

Support for teachers and parents   4

These pages provide teachers and parents with a summary of the key learning in each unit, the vocabulary students will need to become familiar with and some practical ways to reinforce their learning in the classroom and at home.

Unit 1
Number and place value

1A	Place value	15
1B	Rounding	17
1C	Using negative numbers	19
1D	Comparing numbers	21
1E	Using place-value facts	23
	Review	25

Unit 2
Addition, subtraction, multiplication and division

2A	Mental strategies for addition and subtraction	26
2B	Mental strategies for multiplication and division	28
2C	Adding and subtracting near multiples	32
2D	Estimating first in calculations	34
2E	Which operation?	36
2F	Multiplying 3- and 4-digit numbers	38
2G	Long division	40
2H	Short division	42
2I	Division with remainders	44
2J	Factors, multiples and primes	46
2K	Order of operations	48
2L	Using the arithmetical laws	50
	Review	52

Unit 3
Fractions, decimals and percentages

3A	Equivalent fractions	53
3B	Mixed numbers and improper fractions	55
3C	Ordering fractions and mixed numbers	57
3D	Adding and subtracting fractions	59
3E	Multiplying fractions	61
3F	Dividing fractions	63
3G	Fraction and decimal equivalents	65
3H	Place value in decimals	67
3I	Multiplying decimals	69
3J	Dividing decimals	71
3K	Decimal problems	73
3L	Fractions, decimal and percentages	75
	Review	77

Unit 4
Ratio and proportion

4A	Ratio	78
4B	Proportion	80
4C	Percentage problems	82
4D	Scaling problems	84
	Review	86

Unit 5
Algebra

5A Number sequences   87
5B Using a formula   89
5C Missing number problems   91
5D Problems with two unknowns   93
5E Variables   95
Review   97

Unit 6
Length, mass and capacity

6A Comparing units of measure   98
6B Converting units of measure   100
6C Reading scales and measuring accurately   102
6D Imperial units   104
Review   106

Unit 7
Area, perimeter and volume

7A Area and perimeter of rectilinear shapes   107
7B Finding the area of triangles and parallelograms   109
7C Calculating areas of irregular shapes   111
7D Calculating volume   113
Review   115

Unit 8
Time

8A Converting between units of time   116
8B Using the 24-hour clock and timetables   118
8C Time zone problems   120
Review   122

Unit 9
Geometry – properties of shapes

9A Classifying 2D shapes   123
9B Properties of 2D shapes   125
9C Properties of 3D shapes   128
9D Making 2D representations of 3D shapes   130
9E Angles in shapes   132
9F Missing angles   134
9G Circles   136
Review   138

Unit 10
Geometry – position and direction

10A Reading and plotting coordinates   139
10B Translations and reflections   141
Review   143

Unit 11
Statistics

11A Averages   144
11B Probability   146
11C Handling data extended project   148
Review   152

1 Number and place value

What students will learn

This unit further develops students' understanding of place value and number sequences. In the decimal number system, the value of a digit depends on its place, or position, in a number. For example, in the number 8 642 537, the 8 is worth 8 million and the 2 is worth 2 thousand. Students will read, write, order and round numbers up to 10 million. When we work with very large numbers, rounding can help us to make estimates before calculating. Students will also develop their understanding of negative numbers, mainly in the context of temperature.

Finally, they will use all this knowledge to solve real-life problems.

Learning objectives:

- read and compare numbers up to 10 000 000
- round any whole number to a required degree of accuracy
- use negative numbers
- solve number problems.

Key words

place value	greater than (>)	place-value grid
4-, 5-, 6-, 7-digit number	less than (<)	power of 10
multiple of 10	halfway between	positive/negative number
ten thousand, hundred thousand	estimate	number pairs
	approximate	known facts
million, ten million	round to the nearest	derive

Ways to help

- Many people say that when we multiply by 10 we 'add a zero'. This works with whole numbers, but not with decimals. For example, $24.31 \times 100 = 2431$, not 24.3100. Instead, encourage students to use (or imagine) a place-value grid and move the digits two places to the left:

	Thousands	Hundreds	Tens	Ones	.	Tenths	Hundredths
			2	4	.	3	1
× 100	2	4	3	1	.		

- Encourage students to use a number line to help them visualise calculations that go across zero, and say the complete calculation. For example, $25 - 75 = {}^-50$:

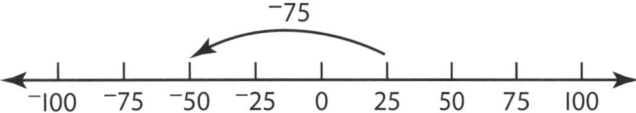

- When you see large numbers in newspapers or magazines, discuss how you could round them to a suitable degree of accuracy.

2 Addition, subtraction, multiplication and division

What students will learn

Mental calculation is one of the most important skills that students can learn. Using known facts to derive new ones is at the heart of problem solving. The first response to any problem should be 'Can I calculate that mentally?' Calculators or a written method should be a last resort. When using these, students should always make an estimate first so that they can check their answer.

Once the firm foundations of mental calculation have been reinforced, students will move on to rehearsing formal written methods for calculating.

Students will also learn about the order of operations, using the acronym 'BIDMAS' as a reminder: brackets, indices, division/multiplication, addition/subtraction.

Learning objectives:

- perform mental calculations, including with mixed operations and large numbers
- use estimation to check answers to calculations
- solve addition, subtraction, multiplication and division problems using written methods
- interpret remainders to division problems as whole number remainders or fractions
- identify common factors, common multiples and prime numbers
- use your knowledge of the order of operations to carry out calculations involving the four operations.

		6	5	4	2
+		3	5	7	3
	1	0	1	1	5
			1	1	

			3	^{1}5	
		5	4̶	6̶	^{1}2
−		3	3	7	7
		2	0	8	5

			3	7	4	2
×						8
		2	9	9	3	6
				5	3	1

					4	6	8
1	2		5	6	^{8}1	^{9}6

Key words

addition	division, divisor	estimate	partition/partitioning
subtraction	dividend	mental strategy/method	recombine
total	remainder		brackets
sum	factor	grid method	order of operations
difference	multiple	column method	BIDMAS
place value	near multiple	written method	commutative law
multiplication	common multiple	long/short multiplication	associative law
multiples of 10	prime number		distributive law
pairs to 10	composite number	long/short division	
product	prime factor	known facts	
quotient	divisibility rules	derive	

Ways to help

- Ask students to explain their strategies. This will help them understand much more clearly how they are approaching calculations, and how to use the same methods for other similar problems.
- Some methods may be different from the ones you were taught at school. Ask students to explain *how* the methods work; this will help them understand the methods better.
- Encourage students always to estimate before calculating. After calculating, remind them to compare their answer to their estimate. If these are very different, students should recheck their work.

3 Fractions, decimals and percentages

What students will learn

The most important thing to understand about fractions is the idea of 'equality' – fractions are 'equal areas' or 'equal shares'. The denominator (bottom number) tells us how many equal parts the whole is divided into. The numerator (top number) tells us how many parts we need to find.

This unit further develops students' understanding of the equivalence between fractions, decimals and percentages. For example, $\frac{3}{4}$ is equivalent to 0.75 and to 75%. Students can then decide which fractional form is the best to use in a particular context.

Students will gain a deeper understanding of fractions greater than 1. These can be written as either improper fractions or mixed numbers. For example, $\frac{7}{4}$ is an improper fraction. The equivalent mixed number is $1\frac{3}{4}$.

Finally, students learn how they can carry out calculations when adding, subtracting, multiplying or dividing fractions and decimals.

Learning objectives:

* use common factors to simplify fractions and use common multiples to write fractions with the same denominator
* compare and order fractions, including fractions greater than 1
* add, subtract, multiply and divide with fractions and decimals
* convert fractions to decimals and decimals to fractions
* understand place value in numbers with up to three decimal places
* solve problems involving fractions, decimals and percentages.

Key words

proper fraction	numerator	decimal equivalent	decimal place
improper fraction	denominator	tenths	round
mixed number	common multiple	nearest tenth	percentages
equivalent fraction	common denominator	hundredths	equivalent
simplest form	decimal fraction	thousandths	bar model

Ways to help

* Students still need to see fractions modelled practically as often as possible, for example by folding paper strips or cutting up cakes or pizzas.
* You could display a fraction wall like this, to help students understand equivalent fractions. Ask students to write the equivalent decimal fractions and percentages on each section of the wall.
* Encourage students to look out for fractions, decimals and percentages in real life. For example, percentages are often used when shops advertise sales, and you could ask students to mentally calculate the new prices.

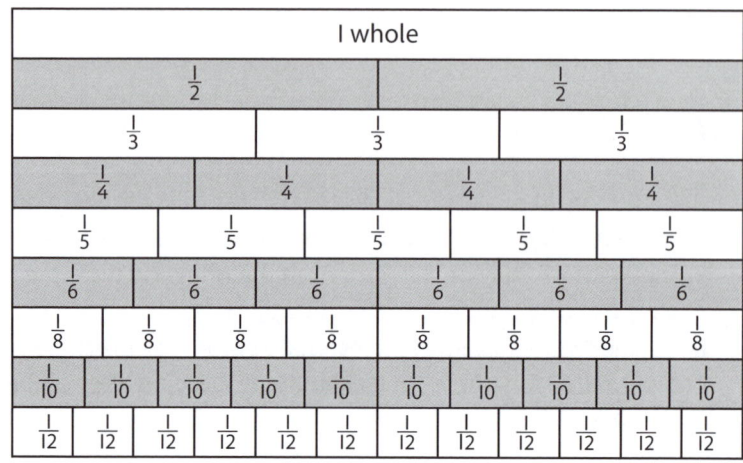

4 Ratio and proportion

What students will learn

In this unit, students use their knowledge of fractions to calculate ratios and proportions.

Ratio compares part to part. For example, 1 to 4 is a ratio. If there is one adult to every four children on a school trip, the ratio of adults to children is 1 : 4. The ratio of children to adults is 4 : 1.

Proportion compares a part to the whole. For example, 1 out of 5 is a proportion. One out of every five people on the trip is an adult. Four out of every five people on the trip are children. Proportions can be expressed as fractions or percentages. For example, $\frac{1}{5}$, or 20%, of the people on the trip are adults; $\frac{4}{5}$, or 80%, of the people on the trip are children.

In this pattern of floor tiles:

- the ratio of black to white tiles is 3 : 7
- the ratio of white to black tiles is 7 : 3.
- the proportion of black tiles is $\frac{3}{10}$, or 30%
- the proportion of white tiles is $\frac{7}{10}$, or 70%.

Learning objectives:

- solve problems using ratio and proportion
- use your knowledge of factors and multiples to solve problems
- solve problems using percentages
- use scale factors to solve problems.

Key words

ratio	percentage decrease
one to four (1 : 4)	scale factor
proportion	enlarge
percentage	enlargement
percentage increase	bar model

Ways to help

- Look in newspapers for reports that use percentages to explain information. Discuss what this means with students.
- Parents/carers: whenever you are using scaling in the home, you could ask students to help. For example, when cooking, students could help to calculate the amount of each ingredient needed for the correct number of people.

5 Algebra

What students will learn

Algebra is used to explore and explain number patterns, but we also use algebra in our day-to-day lives. In this unit, students will create their own number patterns and will find the rules that make the patterns. They will use formulae both from mathematics (for example calculating areas of shapes) and from real life (for example calculating how long a journey will take if we know the speed and the distance to travel).

Students will also begin to solve equations, a skill they will build on in the next phase of their education.

Although this is likely to be the first time students are formally 'introduced' to algebra, they should quickly see the links to work they have done in previous Stages. For example, they will be familiar with missing number problems, such as $92 - ? = 86$. They will encounter similar equations in this unit, with shapes or letters representing the missing numbers.

Learning objectives:

- use simple formulae
- generate and describe linear number sequences
- solve missing number problems
- solve equations with unknown values
- solve problems with variables.

Key words

number sequence	formula, formulae	variable
linear number sequence	equation	constant
rule	missing number	solve
term	unknown	substitute, substitution

Ways to help

- Look out for algebra in real life and involve students in solving problems. If you are planning a trip, use the time/speed/distance formulae to calculate how long it might take. If you have completed a journey, calculate your average speed.

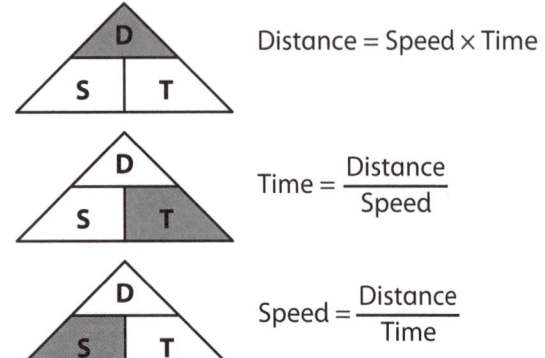

Distance = Speed × Time

$$\text{Time} = \frac{\text{Distance}}{\text{Speed}}$$

$$\text{Speed} = \frac{\text{Distance}}{\text{Time}}$$

6 Length, mass and capacity

What students will learn

By Stage 6, students will have a good understanding of how to measure and compare length, mass and capacity. This unit develops their ability to use their understanding of the decimal number system to convert between metric units. They should remember that, in the context of measures, the prefix 'kilo' means 1000, 'centi' means $\frac{1}{100}$ and 'milli' means $\frac{1}{1000}$.

In this unit students are introduced to the idea that all measurements are approximations. For example, when measuring length we measure to the nearest millimetre, centimetre, metre or kilometre, depending on what we are measuring and the required degree of accuracy.

Students also use imperial units and make approximate conversions to metric units, for example as shown here.

Learning objectives:

- use different units of measure, with up to three decimal places
- convert between different units of measure, with up to three decimal places
- convert between miles and kilometres
- solve measurement problems, including converting between units.

Imperial	Metric (approximate)
1 inch	2.54 centimetres
1 mile	1.6 kilometres
1 pound	0.45 kilograms
1 pint	0.57 litres

Key words

metric unit	millimetre (mm)	imperial unit	gallon
standard unit	tonne (t)	mile	pint
milli-	kilogram (kg)	yard	convert
centi-	gram (g)	foot, feet	conversion graph
kilo-	milligram (mg)	inch	scale drawing
kilometre (km)	litre (ℓ)	stone	degree of accuracy
metre (m)	centilitre (cl)	pound	
centimetre (cm)	millilitre (ml)	ounce	

Ways to help

- As in previous Stages, the best way to reinforce students' measuring skills is to provide lots of opportunities for physical measuring. If you are making something that requires measuring (such as cooking), ask students to carry out the measurements for you.
- Encourage students always to estimate first. This will help to improve their sense of the size of the different units of measurement.

7 Area, perimeter and volume

What students will learn

Students have learned how to calculate area (amount of space covered by a shape) and perimeter (the distance around the edge of a shape) in previous Stages. In this unit, they learn that we use standard measures for these measurements. Perimeter is measured in units of length (for example cm, m, km) and area is measured in square units (for example cm^2, m^2, km^2). This means that we calculate an area by finding out how many unit squares would fit inside the shape.

This unit introduces students to the formulae for calculating areas of parallelograms and triangles.

area of a parallelogram
= base × perpendicular height

area of a triangle
= $\frac{1}{2}$ (base × perpendicular height)

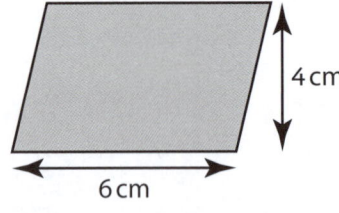

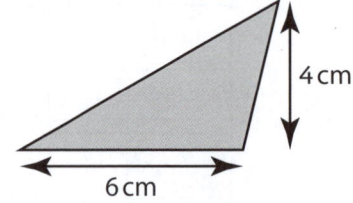

area = 6 × 4 = 24 cm^2

area = $\frac{1}{2}$ (6 × 4) = 12 cm^2

Finally, they will find volumes of a range of containers. Volume is measured in cubic units (for example cm^3, m^3, km^3).

Learning objectives:

- recognise that shapes with the same area can have different perimeters and vice versa
- recognise when it is possible to use formulae to calculate the area and volume of shapes
- calculate the area of parallelograms and triangles
- calculate, estimate and compare the volume of cubes and cuboids.

Key words

perimeter	height	cubic metre (m^3)
area	perpendicular height	rectilinear shape
surface area	base	composite shape
volume	square centimetre (cm^2)	formula
length	square metre (m^2)	tangram
width	cubic centimetre (cm^3)	dimension

Ways to help

- Sometimes students confuse area and perimeter. You can help by looking at shapes and pointing out the perimeter and the area. For example, you could use identical-sized square mats or cards, place them together to make different shapes and ask students to compare the areas and perimeters.
- Ask students to calculate the area and perimeter of rooms at home or at school.
- Ask students to measure the dimensions of packaging boxes to find out the volume.

8 Time

What students will learn

In this unit, students continue to tell the time to the nearest minute using analogue and digital clocks, and using 12-hour and 24-hour time. They will extend their skills in reading timetables and calendars, and carry out calculations involving converting between units of time.

They will be introduced to the concept of time zones and learn how to calculate the time in different places around the world.

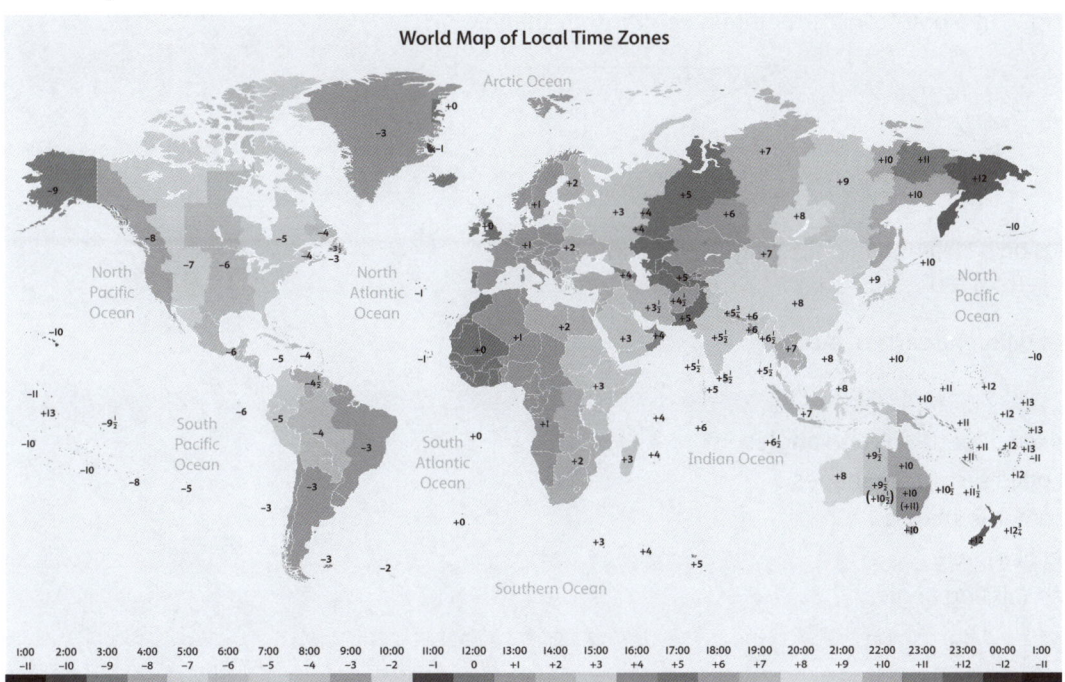

Learning objectives:

- solve problems that involve converting between units of time.

Key words

digital clock	century	hour
analogue clock	decade	second
12-hour clock	year	millisecond
24-hour clock	leap year	timetable
a.m.	month	time zone
p.m.	week	time difference
millennium	day	

Ways to help

- Explore different time zones using the Internet. Find a website that shows clocks telling the time in different cities around the world. If students have family members in other countries, ask them to work out what the time is where their relative lives. For example, at lunchtime ask: 'What time is it where [name of family member] lives? What do you think they are doing now?'

11

9 Geometry – properties of shapes

What students will learn

In this unit, students continue to classify (sort) 2-dimensional (2D) and 3-dimensional (3D) shapes, using increasingly complex properties. They will draw and make 2D and 3D shapes and compare them. By this Stage, students should be able to name all the common 2D and 3D shapes.

They learn how to recognise acute, obtuse and reflex angles, and measure angles to the nearest degree. They use this information to draw shapes accurately. They find missing angles, using their knowledge of the sum of angles at a point, on a straight line and within shapes.

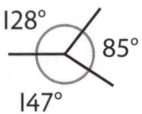

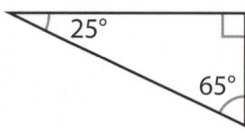

angles at a point
total 360°

angles on a straight line
total 180°

angles in a triangle
total 180°

They also learn the names of different parts of a circle.

Learning objectives:

- draw 2D shapes using given dimensions and angles
- recognise, describe and build simple 3D shapes
- compare and classify geometric shapes
- illustrate and name parts of a circle
- recognise angles and find missing angles.

Key words

2D/3D shape	edge	missing angle	diameter, radius, circumference
polygon	corner	parallel	
polyhedron	vertex, vertices	cube, net of cube	rotational symmetry
regular/irregular	face	dimensions	order of rotational symmetry
properties	right angle	volume	
volume	acute, obtuse, reflex	protractor	isometric paper
side	internal angle	centre	plan
			front/side elevation

Ways to help

- As in the units on shape in earlier Stages, the best way to help students is to point out, name and talk about all the shapes that you see in the environment around you. There will be lots of different shapes at home and in the local area. Take photographs of shapes you see around you and ask students to describe their properties.

10 Geometry – position and direction

What students will learn

This unit develops students' ability to describe the position and movement of objects on coordinate grids, using all four quadrants. We use coordinates to describe position and we use transformations such as reflections, rotations and translations to describe how objects move around the grid.

Learning objectives:

* draw, translate and reflect simple shapes on a coordinate grid
* describe position using all four quadrants on a coordinate grid.

Key words

coordinate grid	origin	mirror line
coordinates	transformation	parallel
axis, axes	translate (slide), translation	perpendicular
quadrants	rotate, rotation	clockwise
first, second, third, fourth quadrant	symmetry, symmetrical	anti-clockwise
	line of symmetry	

Ways to help

* Make copies of a coordinate grid like this one and use cut-out copies of shapes. Students can then physically move the shapes around the grid, giving the coordinates of the vertices and describing the movements. Encourage them to use the correct terminology when they do this.

* Look out for patterns around the home or school that include symmetry and translations. Sketch them on coordinate grids and discuss them.

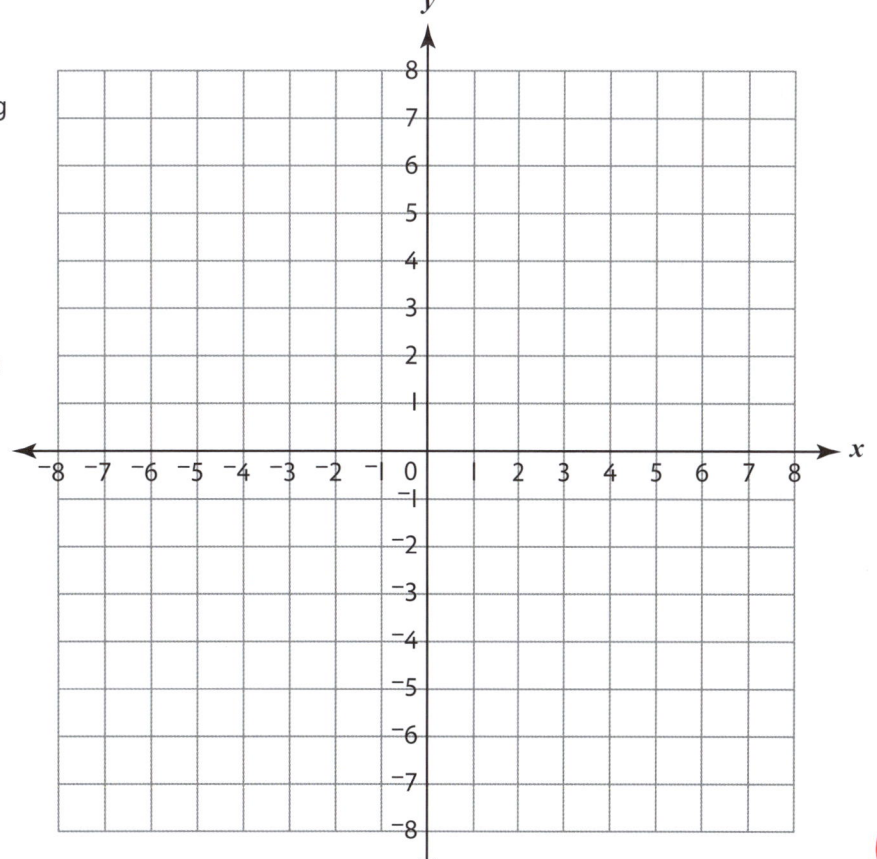

11 Statistics

What students will learn

In this unit, students further develop their understanding of data. They decide on the best type of graph or chart to show different types of data and choose an appropriate scale. The representations focused on in this unit are line graphs and pie charts.

New ideas in this unit include one measure of the 'average' and 'spread' of a set of data, the mean. To calculate the mean average, we add together all the numbers in the set and divide by the quantity in the set. For example, to find the mean of 14, 15, 16, 18, 18, 18, 21, 22, we add all the numbers together and divide by 8:

$$\frac{14 + 15 + 16 + 18 + 18 + 18 + 21 + 22}{8} = \frac{142}{8} = 17.75$$

Students also develop their understanding of probability.

Learning objectives:

- calculate and interpret the mean as an average
- interpret and construct pie charts and line graphs to solve problems.

Key words

data	frequency table	average
continuous data	pie chart	mean
discrete data	line graph	probability
collect, collection	axis, axes	outcome
questionnaire	scale	certain
survey	interval	impossible
research	represent	equally likely
frequency	interpret	equal chance

Ways to help

- Look for graphs and charts presenting data, for example on television, on the Internet and in newspapers. Talk to students about how this data might have been collected and the way it has been represented. Challenge them to work out the mean average of the data where appropriate.
- Carry out data-handling investigations at home or in the classroom, focusing on questions that students are interested in exploring.

1A Place value

Discover   Student Book 6, page 7

Here are some facts from the year 2019.

Write each number in the place-value grid. Say each number aloud.

The first one is done for you.

> The population of Guadalajara, Mexico, was 5 195 534.

Five million, one hundred and ninety-five thousand, five hundred and thirty-four.

1 The world's population grew by about 1 557 692 per week.

2 Roughly 5 595 750 passenger cars were made each month.

3 Every week, approximately 5 019 231 personal computers were sold.

4 Every minute, around 347 222 tweets were sent.

5 The circumference of the Earth at the equator is 40 075 km.

6 At Dubai International Airport there were around 7 199 729 travellers per month.

Millions	Hundred thousands	Ten thousands	Thousands	Hundreds	Tens	Ones
5	1	9	5	5	3	4

Stretch zone

Find a fact about your country that includes a number in the millions.

Write your fact here.

_____

_____

_____

1A Place value

Student Book 6, page 8

Explore

Write four facts about each of these numbers.

Use each word or phrase from the box opposite at least once.

The first two facts are done for you.

- million
- hundred thousand
- ten thousand
- thousand
- hundred
- ten
- one
- is greater than
- is less than
- is approximately

	Number	Facts
1	4 025 680	has zero hundred thousands
		is approximately 4 million
2	7 654 321	
3	555 698	
4	8 945 025	

Stretch zone

Round each number to the nearest 100 000.

Write the rounded numbers in the 'Number' column of the table.

1B Rounding

Discover   Student Book 6, page 9

Follow these steps five times.

- Use these digits to make a 4-digit number.
- Write the thousand before and the thousand after.
- Mark and label the 4-digit number on a number line.
- Round it to the nearest 1000.

The first one is done for you.

| 3 | 5 | 6 | 9 |

Number	The 1000 before	The 1000 after	Number line	The nearest 1000
5693	5000	6000	5693 marked between 5000, 5500 and 6000	6000

Stretch zone

I round a number to the nearest 1 000. The answer is 294 000.

What is the largest number it could have been before rounding?

What is the smallest number it could have been before rounding?

1B Rounding

Explore   Student Book 6, pages 10–12

Use these digits for this activity.

| 4 | 5 | 6 | 7 | 8 | 9 |

I   Use the digits to write nine different 6-digit numbers.
    One is done for you.

456 789				

2   Write your numbers in order in this table, smallest to largest.

- Round to the nearest 10 000 and to the nearest 100 000.

- Find the difference between the two rounded numbers.

Number	Rounded to the nearest 10 000	Rounded to the nearest 100 000	Difference
456 789	460 000	500 000	40 000

Stretch zone

Choose two numbers from the first column of the table. Find the difference between them.

Compare this difference with the differences when the two numbers are rounded to the nearest 10 000 and nearest 100 000.

1C Using negative numbers

Discover Student Book 6, pages 13–14

Average temperatures (°C) each month in Moscow, Reykjavik and the North Pole

Place	Jan	Feb	Mar	Apr	May	Jun	Jul	Aug	Sep	Oct	Nov	Dec
Moscow	-7	-8	-1	7	15	18	21	19	13	6	0	-4
Reykjavik	-5	-3	-3	2	7	8	9	7	5	4	0	-3
North Pole	-25	-19	-14	-10	0	9	13	11	0	-17	-23	-28

Draw the warmest and coldest temperatures for each place on these thermometers.

Moscow		Reykjavik		North Pole	
Warmest	Coldest	Warmest	Coldest	Warmest	Coldest

Stretch zone

Draw a table showing average temperature each month. In the table, write the temperatures where you live, and in a city with very cold winters.

What is the difference in temperature between the hottest month in each city?

What is the difference in temperature between the coldest month in each city?

1C Using negative numbers

Explore   Student Book 6, page 15

Average temperatures (°C) each month in Moscow, Reykjavik and the North Pole

Place	Jan	Feb	Mar	Apr	May	Jun	Jul	Aug	Sep	Oct	Nov	Dec
Moscow	⁻7	⁻8	⁻1	7	15	18	21	19	13	6	0	⁻4
Reykjavik	⁻5	⁻3	⁻3	2	7	8	9	7	5	4	0	⁻3
North Pole	⁻25	⁻19	⁻14	⁻10	0	9	13	11	0	⁻17	⁻23	⁻28

Find the difference between each pair of temperatures.

	Temperature 1	Temperature 2	Difference (°C)
1	coldest month in Moscow	warmest month in Moscow	
2	coldest month in Reykjavik	warmest month in Reykjavik	
3	coldest month at the North Pole	warmest month at the North Pole	
4	coldest month in Moscow	warmest month in Reykjavik	
5	coldest month at the North Pole	warmest month in Moscow	
6	coldest month in Reykjavik	warmest month in Moscow	
7	coldest month at the North Pole	warmest month in Reykjavik	
8	coldest month in Moscow	warmest month at the North Pole	
9	coldest month in Reykjavik	warmest month at the North Pole	

Stretch zone

What is the minimum temperature during the year where you live?   [   ] °C

What is the maximum temperature?   [   ] °C

What is the difference between the minimum and maximum?   [   ] °C

1D Comparing numbers

Discover   Student Book 6, page 16

These are the 2019–2020 annual salaries of some basketball players in the USA.

LeBron James	$37 436 858	Andre Drummond	$27 093 019
Damian Lillard	$29 802 321	Stephen Curry	$40 231 758
Kevin Love	$28 942 830	CJ McCollum	$27 556 959
DeMar DeRozan	$27 739 975	Mike Conley	$32 511 624

- Write them in order in the table, largest to smallest.
- Round each salary to the nearest 100 000.
- Rewrite each rounded amount in the form '$xx.x million'.

The first row is done for you.

	Player	Salary	Rounded to the nearest 100 000	Written as '$xx.x million'
	Stephen Curry	$40 231 758	$40 200 000	$40.2 million
1				
2				
3				
4				
5				
6				
7				

Stretch zone

Research the average salary for a teacher in your country. Convert it to US$.

How many years would the teacher have to work to earn what Stephen Curry earns in one year?

[   ] years

1D Comparing numbers

Explore Student Book 6, page 17

Average low-temperatures in January

	Place	Temperature (°C)
A	International Falls, Minnesota, USA	⁻21 °C
B	Marble Bar, Australia	26 °C
C	Ulaanbaatar, Mongolia	⁻26 °C
D	Barrow, Alaska, USA	⁻29 °C
E	Balikpapan, Indonesia	29 °C
F	Snag, Yukon Territory, Canada	⁻30 °C
G	Bangkok, Thailand	23 °C
H	Verkhoyansk, Russia	⁻48 °C

In the 'Place' row, just write the matching letter (A–H).

1 Write the temperatures in this table, from coldest to warmest.

Place								
Temperature								

2 How much warmer is it in Bangkok than International Falls? ☐ °C

3 How much warmer is it in Marble Bar than International Falls? ☐ °C

4 How much colder is it in Ulaanbaatar than Marble Bar? ☐ °C

5 How much colder is it in Snag than Balikpapan? ☐ °C

Stretch zone

What is the average low-temperature in January where you live? ☐ °C

How much hotter is that than the coldest temperature in the table above? ☐ °C

Discover   Student Book 6, page 18

Use the digits in each number to make number pairs to 100, 10 and 1.

The first one is done for you.

	Number	Addition pair to 100	Addition pair to 10	Addition pair to 1
	38	38 + 62 = 100	3.8 + 6.2 = 10	0.38 + 0.62 = 1
1	85			
2	41			
3	16			
4	73			
5	24			
6	11			
7	89			
8	54			
9	67			
10	14			
11	51			
12	40			
13	5			
14	92			

Stretch zone

Write a rule for using a number pair to 100 to find a number pair to 1.

_____

_____

_____

1E Using place-value facts

Explore   Student Book 6, page 19

Write six number pairs to make each total.

Two pairs are done for you.

	Total	Number pairs		
1	100	$59 + 41 = 100$	$4 + 96 = 100$	
2	1			
3	10			
4	1000			
5	10 000			
6	0.1			
7	0.01			

Stretch zone

You know that $34 + 66 = 100$. How can this fact help you to solve $0.001 - 0.00034$?

_____

_____

_____

1 Number and place value

1 Draw a face next to each bubble to show how confident you feel about your learning.

reading and writing very large numbers

ordering and comparing very large numbers

rounding very large numbers

using negative numbers

2 Tell a partner about one thing you did really well in this unit.

3 Write about what you found easy, what challenged you or what you found really hard.

What work did you feel really confident doing?

_____

_____

_____

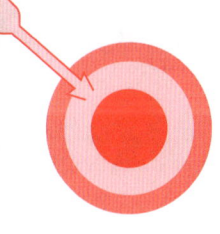

What work really stretched and challenged you?

_____

_____

_____

_____

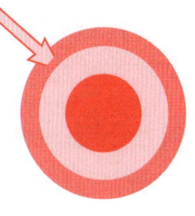

Is there any work you might need some extra help with?

_____

_____

2A Mental strategies for addition and subtraction

Discover
Student Book 6, page 23

Number of people visiting a shop during one week

Day	Number of people
Monday	1452
Tuesday	1378
Wednesday	1650
Thursday	1625
Friday	2175
Saturday	2275
Sunday	49

Solve these problems using mental strategies.

Show your strategies.

1　How many people visited the shop in total on Friday and Saturday?

people

2　How many people visited in total on Monday and Tuesday?

people

3　How many more people visited on Saturday than Sunday?

people

4　How many more people visited on Friday than Thursday?

people

Stretch zone

The owners of the shop aim to have 10 000 people visiting each week.

Do you think they met this target? Use rounding to help you estimate.

Explore   Student Book 6, page 24

For each answer, write five questions.

Some should be additions and some should be subtractions.

> Can you use some very large numbers?
> Can you use some decimals?

1 Answer: 2500

_____

_____

_____

_____

_____

3 Answer: 98

_____

_____

_____

_____

_____

2 Answer: 10 001

_____

_____

_____

_____

_____

4 Answer: 999

_____

_____

_____

_____

_____

Stretch zone

Write a two-step calculation involving addition and subtraction, with the answer 100 501.

_____

Discover 1
Student Book 6, page 25

- digit cards 1–9

Follow these steps for each row of the table.

- Choose five cards. Use some (or all) of the digits to make a number.

- Write a division calculation to match the instruction. Write the answer.

The first one is done for you.

I chose 8, 2, 5, 1, 3. I need to make a number that leaves a remainder when I divide it by 2.

Instruction	Calculation	Answer
division by 2 with a remainder	823 ÷ 2 =	411 r 1
division by 2 with no remainder		
division by 4 with a remainder		
division by 4 with no remainder		
division by 6 with a remainder		
division by 6 with no remainder		
division by 7 with a remainder		
division by 7 with no remainder		
division by 8 with a remainder		
division by 8 with no remainder		
division by 9 with a remainder		
division by 9 with no remainder		
division by 10 with a remainder		
division by 10 with no remainder		

Stretch zone

Write how you know what the remainder will be if you are dividing by 10.

Write how you know what the remainder will be if you are dividing by 5.

2B Mental strategies for multiplication and division

Discover 2   Student Book 6, page 26

Complete this multiplication grid.

×	4	8	16	25	50	150
1	12						
2	13						
3	14						
4	16						
5	18						
6	20						

Write the strategies you used.

Stretch zone

What mental strategy could you use to multiply by 75?

_____

Check your strategy: use it to calculate 75 × 28.

_____

Use a calculator to check your answer. Were you correct? _____

2B Mental strategies for multiplication and division

Explore 1
Student Book 6, page 27

Use your answers in the first grid to help you with the second grid.

Complete these multiplication grids.

×	20	40	30	60	90
1 5					
2 60					
3 70					
4 10					
5 50					

×	20	40	30	60	90
6 9					
7 61					
8 69					
9 11					
10 49					

×	16	25	50	30	60
11 0.1					
12 0.4					
13 0.8					
14 0.2					
15 0.5					

Stretch zone

Use the answers in the grids to solve these calculations.

$5000 \times 600 =$

$69 \times 800 =$

$0.8 \times 900 =$

2B Mental strategies for multiplication and division

Explore 2   Student Book 6, page 28

Complete this diagram with facts you can derive from $21 \times 8 = 168$.

Two are done for you.

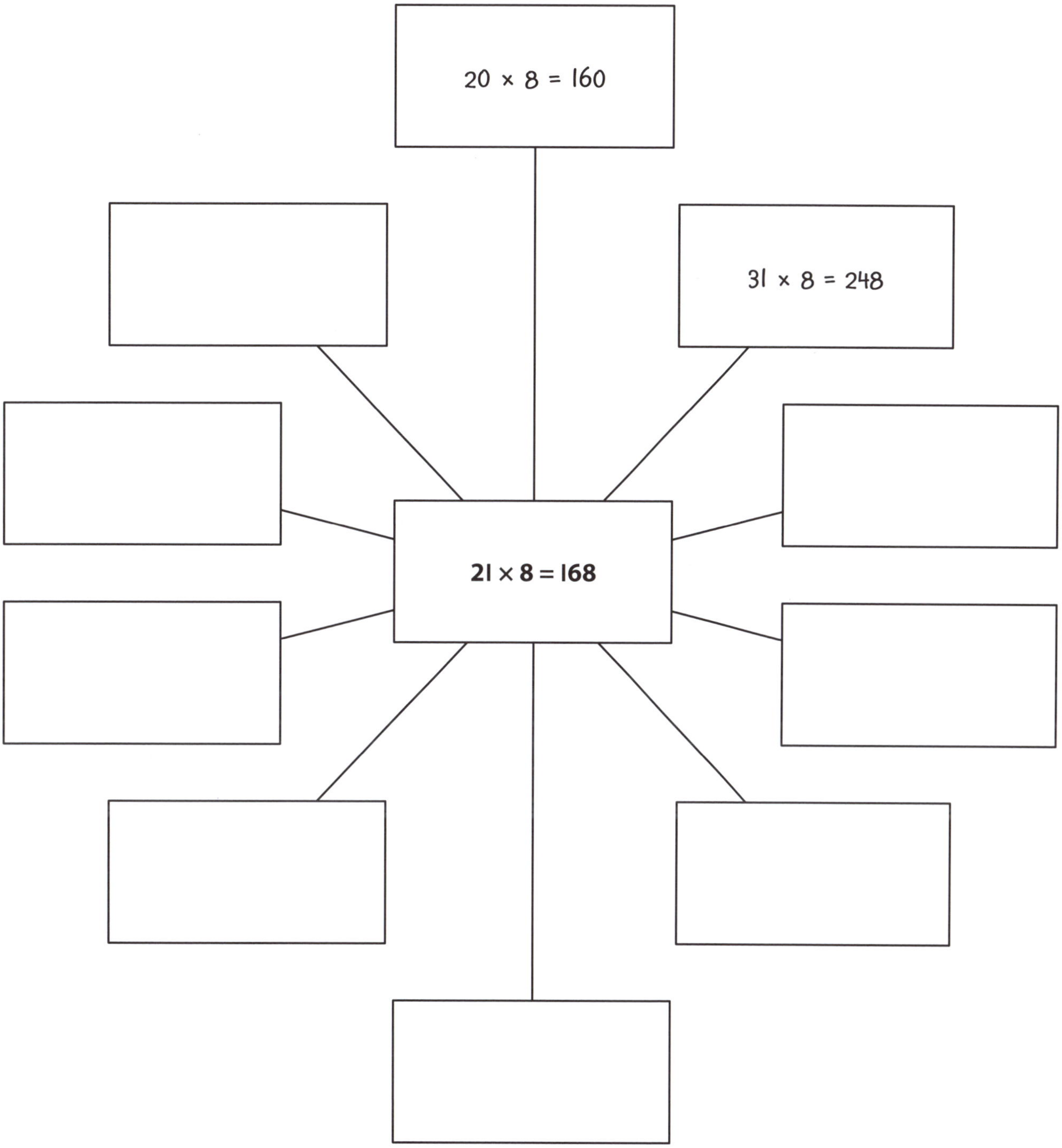

$$20 \times 8 = 160$$

$$31 \times 8 = 248$$

$$21 \times 8 = 168$$

Stretch zone

Draw a similar diagram to show facts derived from 15×17.

2 Addition, subtraction, multiplication and division

31

2C Adding and subtracting near multiples

Discover Student Book 6, page 29

Follow these steps for each row in the table.

- Write a calculation that fits the rules given.
- You must use these six digits.
- Write the missing answer or calculation type.

The first one is done for you.

You do not have to use all the digits for each question.

You can use each digit more than once.

There are lots of possible answers for each question.

	Answer	Calculation type	The calculation must involve:	Calculation
	20	addition	numbers with one place of decimals	9.9 + 10.1
1	20		numbers with one place of decimals	
2	10		numbers with one place of decimals	
3		addition	a near multiple of 100	
4		subtraction	a near multiple of 1000	
5		addition	two 5-digit numbers	
6		subtraction	a 5-digit number and a 4-digit number	
7		multiplication	a near-multiple of 100	
8		multiplication	doubling a number with two places of decimals	

Stretch zone

Write a calculation that involves near multiples, with the answer 25 000.

2C Adding and subtracting near multiples

Explore   Student Book 6, page 30

Price list at a stationery shop

Item	pack of 50 sticky notes	box of 12 pencils	box of 6 pens	pack of printer paper	pack of 5 notebooks
Price	$2.99	$4.98	$4.98	$3.99	$9.98

Calculate the cost of these items. Show your strategies or your workings.

1   5 packs of sticky notes

4   15 notebooks

$ _____

2   5 boxes of pencils

5   24 pencils and 24 pens

$ _____

3   3 packs of printer paper

6   500 sticky notes

$ _____

7   Why do you think so many items in shops are priced at $__.99 or $__.98?

_____

Stretch zone

Sam plans to sell notebooks at school.

How much do you think he should charge for a single notebook? _____

Explain your answer. _____

_____

2D Estimating first in calculations

Discover   Student Book 6, page 31

Solve these calculations.

- Estimate the answer first.

- Decide whether to use a mental or a written method.

- Show your strategies or your workings.

1 175.6 + 28.3 Estimate:	**6** 398 + 146 Estimate:
2 119.7 − 18.4 Estimate:	**7** 965.2 + 425.8 Estimate:
3 210 + 698 Estimate:	**8** 478.6 − 139.8 Estimate:
4 156 + 999 Estimate:	**9** 98.6 − 44.5 Estimate:
5 99.6 − 89.9 Estimate:	**10** 56.88 + 98.75 Estimate:

Stretch zone

Check your answers to **questions 9** and **10** using the inverse operation.

2D Estimating first in calculations

Explore   Student Book 6, page 32

- digit cards 0–9

I chose 1, 7, 4, 8, 9 and 0. I need to aim for an answer of 10.

1 7 4 8 9 0

Follow these steps for each target answer.

- Choose six digit cards.

- Use your digits to write an addition and a subtraction with an answer as close as possible to the target.

- You must use at least four of the digits in each calculation.

- You can use the digits more than once in each calculation.

You will need to use your estimating skills and facts you know.

An example is shown in the table.

My digits	Target answer	Addition	Subtraction
1, 7, 4, 8, 9, 0	10	9.1 + 0.9 = 10	14.8 − 4.8 = 10
	1		
	100		
	1000		
	750		
	75		
	250		
	15.8		
	19.8		
	100.1		

Stretch zone

Use the digits 1, 3, 5, 7 and 9 to make a calculation with the answer 25.
You must use at least three of the digits. You can use the digits more than once.

_____

2E Which operation?

Discover   Student Book 6, page 33

Solve these money word problems.

Read each problem carefully to work out which operation to use.

Show all your workings.

1   I visit a museum with my family and a friend. The family ticket
    costs $28.55. My friend's ticket costs $19.79. What is the total cost?

    $ [   ]

2   My friend and I want to buy a game. The game costs $25. I have $14.67.

    My friend has $8.88. Can we afford the game if we put our money together?

    _____

3   I buy some new clothes for my holiday. I buy two T-shirts for $8.15 each.

    I also buy a pair of shorts for $9.64 and a cap for $2.87. How much do I spend?

    $ [   ]

Stretch zone

Write a word problem using the prices of three items you bought recently.

_____

_____

_____

Ask a partner or an adult to solve your problem. Check their answer.

2E Which operation?

Solve these money word problems.

Read each problem carefully to work out which operations to use.

Show all your workings.

$8.15 $9.64 $2.87

1 I go shopping. I have $25. I buy one of each item above.

How much change do I get?

$ [   ]

2 You plan a class trip to a museum. You collect $175 from the students. The transport costs $88.50.

Entrance costs $65.95. How much do you have left to buy refreshments?

$ [   ]

3 Three classes in your school take part in a sponsored swim.

The three classes raise $42.78, $39.83 and $56.13.

The headteacher has promised to make the amount up to $150.

How much does the headteacher have to pay?

$ [   ]

Stretch zone

Round each of the amounts in **question 3** to the nearest dollar.

If you calculated using the rounded amounts, would the headteacher have to pay more, less or the same amount?

Discover
Student Book 6, pages 35–36

Use partitioning to solve these multiplications. The first one is done for you.

$486 \times 4 = \underline{(400 \times 4) + (80 \times 4) + (6 \times 4) = 1600 + 320 + 24 = 1944}$

1 532×6 _____

2 815×3 _____

3 2268×8 _____

4 5381×6 _____

5 8659×7 _____

Use the grid method to solve these multiplications. The first one is done for you.

$384 \times 26 =$ | 9984

	20	6	
300	6000	1800	7800
80	1600	480	2080
4	80	24	104
			9984

7 $262 \times 53 =$

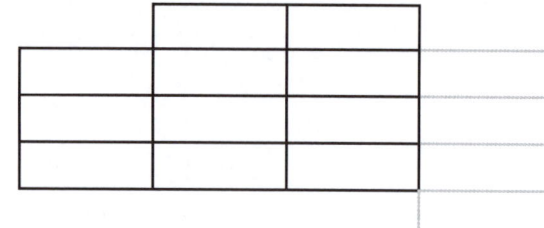

6 $6248 \times 36 =$

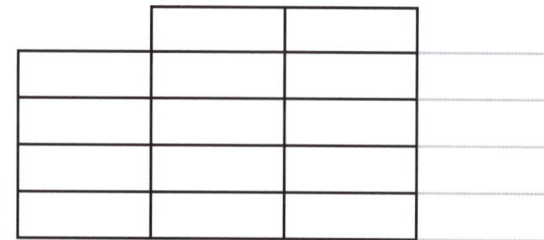

8 $1439 \times 24 =$

Stretch zone

Write a set of instructions to explain how to multiply 472×23 using the grid method.

2F Multiplying 3- and 4-digit numbers

Student Book 6, page 37

Explore

Estimate the answers to these multiplications.

Then use a column method to solve them.

The first one is done for you.

> This method is sometimes called 'long multiplication'.

258×53

Estimate: $250 \times 50 = 12500$

		2	5	8	
×			5	3	
		7	⁷7	⁴4	
1	²2	⁴9	0	0	
1	3	6	7	4	
		1			

1 $298 \times 46 =$

Estimate: _____

2 315×27

Estimate: _____

3 1586×39

Estimate: _____

4 3214×21

Estimate: _____

Stretch zone

Use a mental method to calculate **question 4**.

Could you have used mental methods for any of the other questions?

2G Long division

Discover   Student Book 6, page 38

This is how to use long division to solve 5397 ÷ 21.

2 1 ⑤ 3 9 7	2 1 (⑤) 3 9 7 200 × 21 = 4200 (with 2 above and 4200 below)
Step 1	**Step 2**
Look at the first digit of the dividend (5).	Look at the first two digits instead (53).
How many 21s in 5?	How many 21s in 53?
(We cannot do this, so we move on.)	2 × 21 = 42 (so 200 × 21 = 4200)

Step 1 grid:
```
        2
2 1 | 5 3 9 7
```

Step 2 grid:
```
        2
2 1 | 5 3 9 7
    4 2 0 0        200 × 21 = 4200
```

Step 3 grid:
```
        2
2 1 | 5 3 9 7
  - 4 2 0 0
    1 1 9 7
```

Step 3

Subtract 4200 from the dividend.

5397 − 4200 = 1197

Step 4 grid:
```
        2 5
2 1 | 5 3 9 7
  - 4 2 0 0
   (1 1 9 7)
    1 0 5 0        50 × 21 = 1050
```

Step 4

How many 21s in 119?

5 × 21 = 105 (so 50 × 21 = 1050)

Step 5 grid:
```
        2 5
2 1 | 5 3 9 7
  - 4 2 0 0
    1 1 9 7
  - 1 0 5 0
      1 4 7
```

Step 5

Subtract 1050.

1197 − 1050 = 147

Step 6 grid:
```
        2 5 7
2 1 | 5 3 9 7
  - 4 2 0 0
    1 1 9 7
  - 1 0 5 0
      1 4 7        7 × 21 = 147
```

Step 6

How many 21s in 147?

7 × 21 = 147

There is no remainder. So **5397 ÷ 21 = 257**.

 Use the long division method to solve these divisions. Estimate first.

1   3795 ÷ 11   **2**   2790 ÷ 15   **3**   4944 ÷ 12   **4**   4656 ÷ 16

Stretch zone

 Write a division with a 4-digit dividend and a 2-digit divisor greater than 20.
Solve it using long division.

2G Long division

Estimate the answers to these divisions.

Then use the long division method to solve them.

The first one is done for you.

$9136 \div 16$

Estimate: $9000 \div 15 = 600$

```
          5  7  1
   1  6 | 9  1  3  6
      -  8  0  0  0    500 × 16 = 8000
            1  1  3  6
         -  1  1  2  0    70 × 16 = 1120
                  1  6    1 × 16 = 16
```

$9136 \div 16 = \boxed{571}$

1 $544 \div 17$

Estimate: _____

$544 \div 17 = \boxed{}$

2 $882 \div 14$

Estimate: _____

$882 \div 14 = \boxed{}$

3 $7540 \div 13$

Estimate: _____

$7540 \div 13 = \boxed{}$

4 $6876 \div 18$

Estimate: _____

$6876 \div 18 = \boxed{}$

Stretch zone

Write a division of a 3-digit number by a 2-digit number that you think will have an answer close to 17. Carry out the calculation to check.

2H Short division

Discover Student Book 6, page 40

This is how to use short division to solve 5388 ÷ 12.

1 2 ⑤ 3 8 8		

Step 1

Look at the first digit of the dividend (5).

How many 12s in 5?

(We cannot do this, so we move on.)

⠀⠀⠀⠀4		
1 2 ⑤ 3 8 8		

Step 2

Look at the first two digits instead (53).

How many 12s in 53?

$4 \times 12 = 48$

⠀⠀⠀⠀4		
1 2 5 3 ^{5}8 8		

Step 3

Carry the remainder over to the next digit.

$53 - 48 = 5$

⠀⠀⠀⠀4 4		
1 2 5 3 ⑤^{5}8 8		

Step 4

How many 12s in 58?

$4 \times 12 = 48$

⠀⠀⠀⠀4 4		
1 2 5 3 ^{5}8 ^{10}8		

Step 5

Carry the remainder over to the next digit.

$58 - 48 = 10$

⠀⠀⠀⠀4 4 9		
1 2 5 3 ^{5}8 ^{10}8		

Step 6

How many 12s in 108?

$9 \times 12 = 108$

There is no remainder. So **5388 ÷ 12 = 449**.

 Use the short division method to solve these divisions. Estimate first.

1 6682 ÷ 13 **2** 2464 ÷ 14 **3** 5871 ÷ 19 **4** 3278 ÷ 22

Stretch zone

Find the missing digits in this short division.

```
      1 ☐ 4 r 3
1 1 ⟌ ☐ 8 0 ☐
```

2H Short division

Explore   Student Book 6, page 41

Solve these problems.

Show all your workings.

Show that you are correct using short division.

1   ☐ ☐ ☐ ÷ ☐ ☐ = 39

The missing digits are 1, 1, 2, 8, 9.

2   ☐ ☐ ☐ ÷ ☐ ☐ = 52

The missing digits are 1, 4, 7, 8, 8.

3   ☐ ☐ ☐ ÷ ☐ ☐ = 63

The missing digits are 1, 4, 5, 5, 9.

4   ☐ ☐ ☐ ÷ ☐ ☐ = 71

The missing digits are 1, 2, 3, 3, 9.

Stretch zone

Write a 4-digit number that you know will divide by 9 without leaving a remainder. ☐

Check by carrying out the calculation using short division.

21 Division with remainders

Discover
Student Book 6, pages 42–43

Solve these divisions.

Give each answer as a mixed number and as a decimal number.

The first one is done for you.

Remember:

$\frac{1}{10} = 0.1$ $\qquad$ $\frac{1}{4} = 0.25$

$\frac{1}{5} = 0.2$ $\qquad$ $\frac{1}{8} = 0.125$

$\frac{1}{3} = 0.\dot{3}$

$56 \div 5 = 11$ remainder 1

$\qquad = 11\frac{1}{5} = 11.2$

1 $79 \div 4 =$

2 $158 \div 6 =$

3 $43 \div 3 =$

4 $83 \div 8 =$

5 $69 \div 6 =$

6 $128 \div 12 =$

7 $56 \div 9 =$

8 $327 \div 5 =$

9 $199 \div 8 =$

10 $1410 \div 12 =$

Stretch zone

Write a number > 1410 that will divide by 12 without leaving a remainder.

Use your answer to **question 10** to help you.

_____

21 Division with remainders

Explore   Student Book 6, pages 44–45

Solve these problems.

You will need to round each answer.

1   A pack of 6 bottles of juice costs $9.09.

How much does each bottle cost, to the nearest cent?

$[   ]

2   A pack of 8 bottles of juice costs $10.76.

How much does each bottle cost, to the nearest cent?

$[   ]

3   Approximately how much do I save per bottle of juice if I buy a pack of 8 rather than a pack of 6?

$[   ]

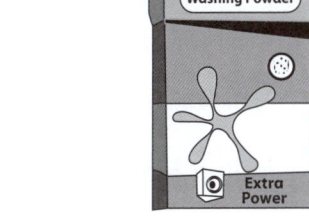

4   Washing powder costs $12.87 for 9 kg.

How much does 1 kg cost, to the nearest 10 cents?

$[   ]

5   A 4 kg box of washing powder costs $6.44.

How much does 1 kg cost, to the nearest 10 cents?

$[   ]

Stretch zone

You want to sell bottles of juice at a charity stall.

You buy 80 bottles of juice in packs of 8 ($10.76 per pack).

At what price would you sell each bottle of juice? Explain your answer.

2J Factors, multiples and primes

Discover   Student Book 6, pages 46–47

Find the lowest common multiple of each pair of numbers by listing the multiples.

The first one is done for you.

The lowest common multiple of 4 and 15 is $\boxed{60}$.

multiples of 4:   4, 8, 12, 16, 20, 24, 28, 32, 36, 40, 44, 48, 52, 56, 60 ...

multiples of 15:   15, 30, 45, 60 ...

1 The lowest common multiple of 5 and 11 is $\boxed{}$.

multiples of 5: _____

multiples of 11: _____

2 The lowest common multiple of 6 and 16 is $\boxed{}$.

multiples of 6: _____

multiples of 16: _____

3 The lowest common multiple of 7 and 13 is $\boxed{}$.

multiples of 7: _____

multiples of 13: _____

4 The lowest common multiple of 6 and 19 is $\boxed{}$.

multiples of 6: _____

multiples of 19: _____

5 The lowest common multiple of 7 and 14 is $\boxed{}$.

multiples of 7: _____

multiples of 14: _____

6 The lowest common multiple of 8 and 12 is $\boxed{}$.

multiples of 8: _____

multiples of 12: _____

Stretch zone

True or false? To find the lowest common multiple of two numbers you multiply them together. Explain your answer using examples.

2J Factors, multiples and primes

Explore
Student Book 6, pages 48–49

Draw a factor tree to find the prime factors of each number.

A prime number has only two factors: itself and I.

A prime factor is a factor that is a prime number.

A factor tree can help you to find all the prime factors of a number.

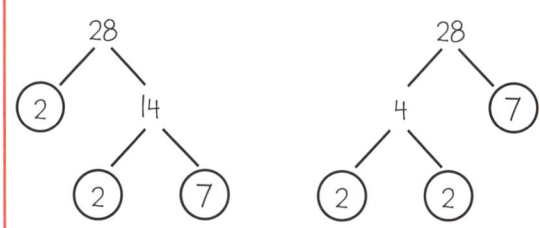

Example

There are two possible factor trees for 28:

The prime factors of 28 are 2, 2 and 7.

28 = 2 × 2 × 7

I 60

4 36

7 64

2 85

5 72

8 87

3 52

6 90

9 50

Stretch zone

One of the numbers above has a factor tree with 8 branches.

Can you find another number with a factor tree that has 8 branches?

2K Order of operations

Discover   Student Book 6, page 50

Make eight different pairs of calculations, using:

- brackets
- any of the operations (=, −, ×, ÷)
- the digits 2, 3, 4 and 5.

You cannot repeat a digit in a calculation.

You can make 1-digit and 2-digit numbers.

For each pair of calculations, use the digits and operations in the same order, but place the brackets to give each calculation a different answer.

Two examples are shown below.

	Calculation 1	Answer 1	Calculation 2	Answer 2
	(2 + 3) × (4 + 5) =	45	2 + (3 × 4) + 5 =	19
	(43 + 2) ÷ 5 =	9	43 + (2 ÷ 5) =	43.4
1				
2				
3				
4				
5				
6				
7				
8				

Stretch zone

What is the largest total you could make? _____

What is the smallest total you could make? _____

Write the calculations as well as the answers.

2K Order of operations

Student Book 6, page 51

Explore

This Practice Book was published in 2021.

Use the digits 2, 0, 2, 1 and the rules for order of operations to make as many numbers between 1 and 20 as you can.

You cannot repeat a digit in a calculation.

You can make 1-, 2- or 3-digit numbers.

Remember:

you can use 'BIDMAS' to help you remember the order of operations.

BIDMAS

( ) x^y ÷ or × + or −

Brackets   Indices Divide and Multiply   Add and Subtract

The first one is done for you.

Calculation	Answer
22 × 0 + 1 =	1
=	2
=	3
=	4
=	5
=	6
=	7
=	8
=	9
=	10

Calculation	Answer
=	11
=	12
=	13
=	14
=	15
=	16
=	17
=	18
=	19
=	20

Stretch zone

How close to the date of your birthday can you get using the digits 1, 9, 8, 3?

For example, if you were born on 15 September, you would try to make an answer of 15.

You cannot repeat a digit in your calculation. You can make 1-, 2- or 3-digit numbers.

2L Using the arithmetical laws

Discover   Student Book 6, page 52

Solve these multiplications.

Use the **commutative law** to make them easier to solve.

The first one is done for you.

20 × 18 × 5

= 20 × 5 × 18

= 100 × 18 = 1800

4 5 × 36 × 5

8 19 × 25 × 4

1 17 × 25 × 4

5 20 × 16 × 5

9 8 × 15 × 2

2 50 × 26 × 2

6 5 × 38 × 2

10 4 × 29 × 25

3 30 × 14 × 3

7 14 × 60 × 10

11 2 × 38 × 50

Stretch zone

How many different ways can you reorder a multiplication of three numbers?

(You could also think about breaking one or more of the numbers into factors.)

Choose a multiplication. See how many different ways you can write it.

2L Using the arithmetical laws

Solve these multiplications.

Use the **distributive law** to make them easier to solve.

The first one is done for you.

62 × 9

= (60 × 9) + (2 × 9)

= 540 + 18 = 558

4   36 × 7

8   37 × 8

1   74 × 3

5   82 × 4

9   46 × 7

2   86 × 5

6   99 × 7

10   37 × 9

3   29 × 6

7   26 × 8

11   82 × 6

Stretch zone

Look at **question 3**. Do you think the distributive law is the best way to calculate this?

Would another method be more efficient? Explain your answer.

_____

_____

Review

I Draw a face next to each bubble to show how confident you feel about your learning.

mental calculation strategies

written calculation methods

factors, multiples and prime numbers

the order of operations

solving calculation problems

 2 Tell a partner about one thing you did really well in this unit.

3 Write about what you found easy, what challenged you or what you found really hard.

What work did you feel really confident doing?

_____

_____

_____

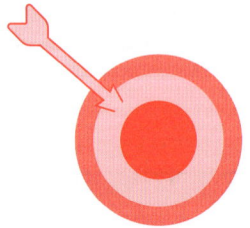

What work really stretched and challenged you?

_____

_____

_____

_____

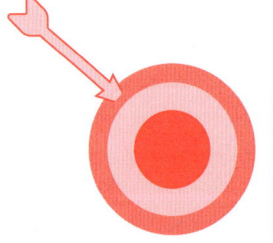

Is there any work you might need some extra help with?

_____

_____

3A Equivalent fractions

Discover
Student Book 6, page 58

Draw bar models to check whether these fractions are equivalent.

Circle **equivalent** or **not**.

The first one is done for you.

● a ruler

$\frac{3}{5}$ and $\frac{6}{10}$ (I multiplied the numerator and denominator by 2)   (equivalent) / not

1 $\frac{2}{3}$ and $\frac{6}{9}$ (I multiplied the numerator and denominator by 3)   equivalent / not

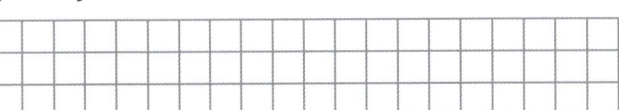

2 $\frac{3}{5}$ and $\frac{7}{8}$ (I added 4 to the numerator and denominator)   equivalent / not

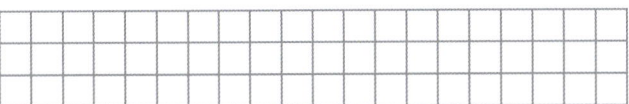

3 $\frac{3}{4}$ and $\frac{6}{8}$ (I doubled the numerator and denominator)   equivalent / not

4 $\frac{10}{12}$ and $\frac{6}{8}$ (I subtracted 4 from the numerator and denominator)   equivalent / not

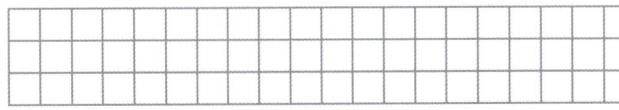

5 $\frac{15}{18}$ and $\frac{5}{6}$ (I divided the numerator and denominator by 3)   equivalent / not

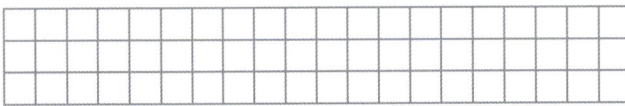

Stretch zone

 Write a rule for finding equivalent fractions.

3A Equivalent fractions

Explore
Student Book 6, page 59

For each fraction write four equivalent fractions.

The last fraction in each set should be in the simplest form.

The first one is done for you.

	Fraction	Equivalent fractions			
	$\frac{150}{180}$	$\frac{15}{18}$	$\frac{30}{36}$	$\frac{10}{12}$	$\frac{5}{6}$
1	$\frac{100}{200}$				
2	$\frac{75}{100}$				
3	$\frac{40}{60}$				
4	$\frac{200}{500}$				
5	$\frac{160}{200}$				
6	$\frac{140}{200}$				
7	$\frac{90}{240}$				
8	$\frac{80}{280}$				

Stretch zone

Write how you know when a fraction is in its simplest form.

_____

_____

_____

3B Mixed numbers and improper fractions

Discover Student Book 6, page 60

Write these improper fractions as mixed numbers.

1 $\dfrac{9}{2} = $ ☐

5 $\dfrac{9}{4} = $ ☐

2 $\dfrac{17}{4} = $ ☐

6 $\dfrac{11}{6} = $ ☐

3 $\dfrac{16}{5} = $ ☐

7 $\dfrac{25}{8} = $ ☐

4 $\dfrac{23}{5} = $ ☐

8 $\dfrac{31}{10} = $ ☐

> Remember:
>
> divide the numerator by the denominator and write the remainder as a fraction.
>
> For example:
>
> $\dfrac{13}{3} = 4\dfrac{1}{3}$, because $13 \div 3 = 4$ remainder 1

Write these mixed numbers as improper fractions.

9 $3\dfrac{1}{4} = $ ☐

13 $1\dfrac{9}{10} = $ ☐

10 $4\dfrac{1}{8} = $ ☐

14 $10\dfrac{1}{8} = $ ☐

11 $4\dfrac{3}{8} = $ ☐

15 $6\dfrac{4}{5} = $ ☐

12 $5\dfrac{2}{9} = $ ☐

16 $3\dfrac{9}{11} = $ ☐

> Remember:
>
> multiply the whole number by the denominator, then add the fractional part.
>
> For example:
>
> $4\dfrac{3}{5} = \dfrac{23}{5}$, because $(4 \times 5) + 3 = 23$.

Stretch zone

Draw a diagram to show an improper fraction less than $3\dfrac{3}{4}$.

Write it as an improper fraction and a mixed number.

3B Mixed numbers and improper fractions

Explore
Student Book 6, pages 61–62

Complete the table.

Write a suitable improper fraction and equivalent mixed number each time.

The first one is done for you.

	Instruction	Mixed number	Improper fraction
1	a fraction bigger than 3	$4\frac{2}{5}$	$\frac{22}{5}$
2	a fraction bigger than 5		
3	a fraction smaller than 7		
4	a fraction between 7 and 9		
5	a fraction bigger than $5\frac{2}{5}$		
6	a fraction smaller than $4\frac{3}{4}$		
7	a fraction bigger than $10\frac{3}{5}$		
8	a fraction between 8 and 9		
9	a fraction bigger than 15		
10	a fraction between $6\frac{1}{2}$ and $6\frac{3}{4}$		

 **Stretch zone**

Choose five of the fractions above. Write them in order, smallest to largest.

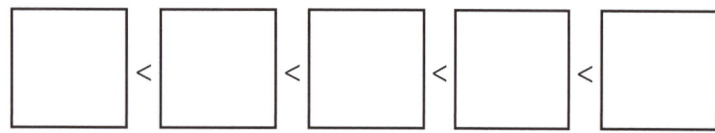

Discover

Student Book 6, page 63

Compare the fractions in each pair.

Write the fractions with < or > between them.

Then write the fractions in their simplest forms with < or > between them.

Show your workings.

The first one is done for you.

$\frac{3}{6}$ and $\frac{2}{12}$

$\frac{3}{6} = \frac{6}{12}$

$\frac{6}{12} > \frac{2}{12}$

$\frac{3}{6} > \frac{2}{12}$

$\frac{1}{2} > \frac{1}{6}$

I whole														

Fraction wall rows:
I whole
$\frac{1}{2}$ $\frac{1}{2}$
$\frac{1}{3}$ $\frac{1}{3}$ $\frac{1}{3}$
$\frac{1}{4}$ $\frac{1}{4}$ $\frac{1}{4}$ $\frac{1}{4}$
$\frac{1}{5}$ $\frac{1}{5}$ $\frac{1}{5}$ $\frac{1}{5}$ $\frac{1}{5}$
$\frac{1}{6}$ $\frac{1}{6}$ $\frac{1}{6}$ $\frac{1}{6}$ $\frac{1}{6}$ $\frac{1}{6}$
$\frac{1}{7}$ $\frac{1}{7}$ $\frac{1}{7}$ $\frac{1}{7}$ $\frac{1}{7}$ $\frac{1}{7}$ $\frac{1}{7}$
$\frac{1}{8}$ $\frac{1}{8}$ $\frac{1}{8}$ $\frac{1}{8}$ $\frac{1}{8}$ $\frac{1}{8}$ $\frac{1}{8}$ $\frac{1}{8}$
$\frac{1}{9}$ $\frac{1}{9}$ $\frac{1}{9}$ $\frac{1}{9}$ $\frac{1}{9}$ $\frac{1}{9}$ $\frac{1}{9}$ $\frac{1}{9}$ $\frac{1}{9}$
$\frac{1}{10}$ ×10
$\frac{1}{11}$ ×11
$\frac{1}{12}$ ×12
$\frac{1}{13}$ ×13
$\frac{1}{14}$ ×14
$\frac{1}{15}$ ×15
$\frac{1}{16}$ ×16

1. $\frac{3}{4}$ and $\frac{3}{8}$

2. $\frac{2}{5}$ and $\frac{5}{10}$

3. $\frac{8}{14}$ and $\frac{3}{7}$

4. $\frac{9}{13}$ and $\frac{4}{9}$

5. $\frac{5}{15}$ and $\frac{3}{6}$

6. $\frac{8}{16}$ and $\frac{3}{8}$

Stretch zone

Write three fractions between $\frac{1}{2}$ and $\frac{3}{4}$. ☐ ☐ ☐

Write them in their simplest forms, in order from smallest to largest. ☐ < ☐ < ☐

3 Fractions, decimals and percentages

Explore
Student Book 6, page 64

Follow these steps for each question.

- Decide how to label the start and end of the number line.

- Write four fractions in the given range. Choose fractions that will fit on one of the marked divisions.

- Mark the position of your four fractions on the number line.

- Label the fractions as mixed numbers above the line.

- Label the fractions as improper fractions below the line.

The first one is done for you.

four fractions between $1\frac{1}{2}$ and $2\frac{1}{2}$

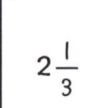 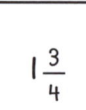

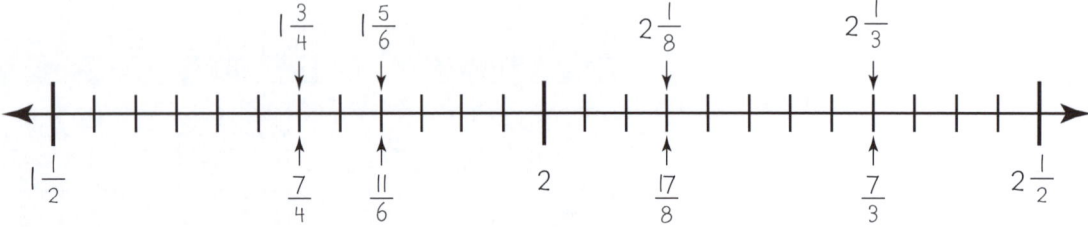

I four fractions between 3 and 4

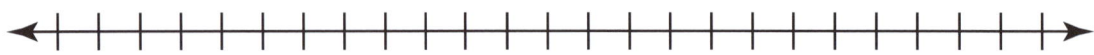

2 four fractions between $8\frac{1}{2}$ and 9

Stretch zone

 Repeat as above, with four fractions between $2\frac{1}{2}$ and $2\frac{3}{4}$. Draw your own number line.

3D Adding and subtracting fractions

Discover Student Book 6, page 65

Complete the second fraction in each addition and write the answer.

- The total should be as close to 1 as possible.
- The total cannot be exactly 1.
- The total cannot be greater than 1.

1 $\frac{1}{2} + \boxed{\frac{}{8}} = \boxed{}$

2 $\frac{1}{2} + \boxed{\frac{}{10}} = \boxed{}$

3 $\frac{1}{2} + \boxed{\frac{}{12}} = \boxed{}$

4 $\frac{1}{2} + \boxed{} = \boxed{}$

5 $\frac{1}{3} + \boxed{\frac{}{6}} = \boxed{}$

6 $\frac{1}{3} + \boxed{\frac{}{9}} = \boxed{}$

7 $\frac{1}{3} + \boxed{\frac{}{12}} = \boxed{}$

8 $\frac{1}{3} + \boxed{} = \boxed{}$

9 $\frac{1}{4} + \boxed{\frac{}{8}} = \boxed{}$

10 $\frac{1}{4} + \boxed{\frac{}{12}} = \boxed{}$

11 $\frac{1}{4} + \boxed{\frac{}{16}} = \boxed{}$

12 $\frac{1}{4} + \boxed{} = \boxed{}$

13 $\frac{1}{5} + \boxed{\frac{}{10}} = \boxed{}$

14 $\frac{1}{5} + \boxed{\frac{}{15}} = \boxed{}$

15 $\frac{1}{5} + \boxed{\frac{}{20}} = \boxed{}$

16 $\frac{1}{5} + \boxed{} = \boxed{}$

Stretch zone

Write an addition with the answer $\frac{19}{20}$.

One of the fractions should have a denominator that is not 20.

$\boxed{} + \boxed{} = \boxed{}$

3D Adding and subtracting fractions

Explore   Student Book 6, page 66

Complete the second fraction in each subtraction and write the answer.

- The answer should be as close to 0 as possible.
- The answer cannot be exactly 0.
- The answer cannot be less than 0.

1 $\frac{1}{2} - \frac{}{8} = \boxed{}$

2 $\frac{1}{2} - \frac{}{10} = \boxed{}$

3 $\frac{1}{2} - \frac{}{12} = \boxed{}$

4 $\frac{1}{2} - \boxed{} = \boxed{}$

5 $\frac{1}{3} - \frac{}{6} = \boxed{}$

6 $\frac{1}{3} - \frac{}{9} = \boxed{}$

7 $\frac{1}{3} - \frac{}{12} = \boxed{}$

8 $\frac{1}{3} - \boxed{} = \boxed{}$

9 $\frac{1}{4} - \frac{}{8} = \boxed{}$

10 $\frac{1}{4} - \frac{}{12} = \boxed{}$

11 $\frac{1}{4} - \frac{}{16} = \boxed{}$

12 $\frac{1}{4} - \boxed{} = \boxed{}$

13 $\frac{1}{5} - \frac{}{10} = \boxed{}$

14 $\frac{1}{5} - \frac{}{15} = \boxed{}$

15 $\frac{1}{5} - \frac{}{20} = \boxed{}$

16 $\frac{1}{5} - \boxed{} = \boxed{}$

Stretch zone

Write a subtraction with the answer $\frac{1}{20}$.

One of the fractions should have a denominator that is not 20.

$\boxed{} - \boxed{} = \boxed{}$

3E Multiplying fractions

Discover   Student Book 6, page 67

Shade squares in the grids to solve these multiplications.

Write the answers in the simplest form.

The first one is done for you.

On this page, $\frac{1}{4} \times \frac{2}{5}$ means the same as $\frac{1}{4}$ **of** $\frac{2}{5}$.

$$\frac{1}{4} \times \frac{2}{5} = \frac{2}{20} = \frac{1}{10}$$

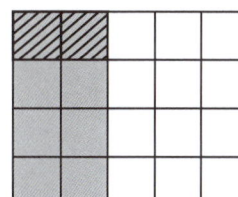

1 $\frac{1}{2} \times \frac{2}{5} =$

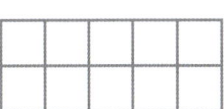

2 $\frac{1}{3} \times \frac{2}{5} =$

3 $\frac{2}{3} \times \frac{2}{5} =$

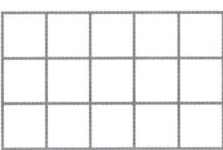

4 $\frac{2}{3} \times \frac{1}{2} =$

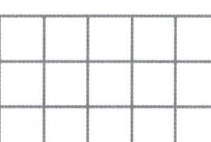

5 $\frac{2}{3} \times \frac{3}{5} =$

6 $\frac{1}{6} \times \frac{1}{2} =$

Stretch zone

Look at the answers.

Write a method for multiplying fractions without drawing a diagram.

3E Multiplying fractions

Explore   Student Book 6, page 68

Solve these fraction multiplications.

Give the answers in the simplest form.

Example $\frac{3}{4} \times \frac{2}{9}$
Multiply the numerators: $3 \times 2 = 6$
Multiply the denominators: $4 \times 9 = 36$
So $\frac{3}{4} \times \frac{2}{9} = \frac{6}{36}$
Simplest form: $\frac{6}{36} = \frac{1}{6}$

	a	b	c
1	$\frac{1}{6} \times \frac{1}{4}$	$\frac{1}{6} \times \frac{1}{2}$	$\frac{1}{6} \times \frac{3}{4}$
2	$\frac{2}{3} \times \frac{1}{4}$	$\frac{2}{3} \times \frac{1}{2}$	$\frac{2}{3} \times \frac{3}{4}$
3	$\frac{3}{4} \times \frac{1}{4}$	$\frac{3}{4} \times \frac{1}{2}$	$\frac{3}{4} \times \frac{3}{4}$
4	$\frac{5}{6} \times \frac{1}{4}$	$\frac{5}{6} \times \frac{1}{2}$	$\frac{5}{6} \times \frac{3}{4}$
5	$\frac{1}{3} \times \frac{1}{5}$	$\frac{1}{3} \times \frac{2}{5}$	$\frac{1}{3} \times \frac{3}{5}$

Stretch zone

 Write two things you notice about the patterns in your answers.

3F Dividing fractions

Discover   Student Book 6, page 69

Solve these fraction divisions.

Shade the diagrams to help you.

Write the answers in the simplest form.

The first one is done for you.

$\frac{2}{3} \div 2 = \frac{2}{6} = \frac{1}{3}$

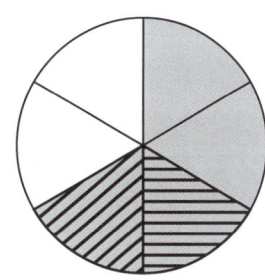

1 $\frac{2}{3} \div 3 =$

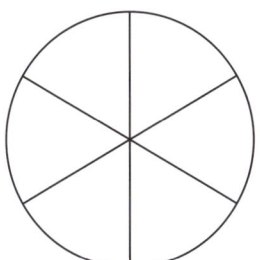

2 $\frac{1}{3} \div 3 =$

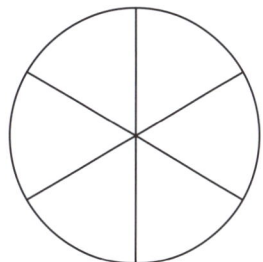

3 $\frac{5}{6} \div 3 =$

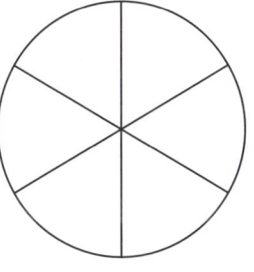

4 $\frac{5}{6} \div 2 =$

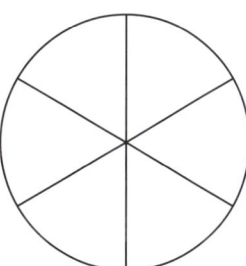

5 $\frac{1}{2} \div 2 =$

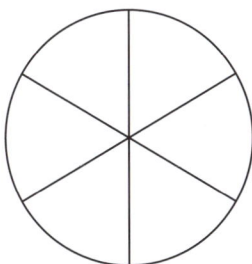

6 $\frac{1}{2} \div 3 =$

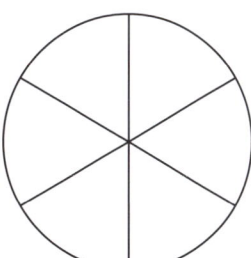

Stretch zone

 Write two things you notice about your answers.

Explore

Student Book 6, page 70

Solve these fraction divisions.

Draw bar models help you.

The first one is done for you.

	Division	Bar model	Answer
	$\frac{1}{3} \div 4$	$\frac{1}{3}$ $\frac{1}{3}$ $\frac{1}{3}$ / $\frac{1}{12}$ $\frac{1}{12}$ $\frac{1}{12}$ $\frac{1}{12}$ $\frac{1}{12}$ $\frac{1}{12}$ $\frac{1}{12}$ $\frac{1}{12}$ $\frac{1}{12}$ $\frac{1}{12}$ $\frac{1}{12}$ $\frac{1}{12}$	$\frac{1}{12}$
1	$\frac{1}{3} \div 2$		
2	$\frac{1}{3} \div 3$		
3	$\frac{1}{3} \div 5$		
4	$\frac{2}{3} \div 2$		
5	$\frac{2}{3} \div 3$		
6	$\frac{2}{3} \div 4$		

Stretch zone

 Rewrite your answers in the following form.

There are 4 lots of $\frac{1}{12}$ in $\frac{1}{3}$.

3G Fraction and decimal equivalents

Discover
Student Book 6, page 71

Match these decimals to their equivalent fractions.

Draw lines to join the pairs.

The first one is done for you.

Match the pairs you are certain of first.

Then use those answers to help you work out others. For example:

I know that $\frac{1}{10} = 0.1$. I know that $\frac{1}{5}$ is the same as $\frac{2}{10}$.

So $\frac{1}{5}$ must be equivalent to 0.2.

	$\frac{1}{10}$	0.2
1	$\frac{3}{8}$	0.375
2	$\frac{1}{2}$	0.6
3	$\frac{5}{8}$	0.125
4	$\frac{3}{4}$	0.625
5	$\frac{1}{5}$	0.75
6	$\frac{3}{5}$	0.9
7	$\frac{9}{10}$	0.1
8	$\frac{1}{4}$	0.25
9	$\frac{1}{8}$	0.5

Stretch zone

Write two ways of knowing that $\frac{3}{8}$ is less than $\frac{1}{2}$.

_____

_____

3G Fraction and decimal equivalents

Explore

Student Book 6, page 72

Convert these fractions into decimals. Show your workings.

Two are done for you.

	Fraction	Decimal	Workings
	$\frac{1}{20}$	0.05	$\frac{1}{10} = 0.1$ $\frac{1}{20}$ is half of $\frac{1}{10}$ so $\frac{1}{20} = 0.05$
1	$\frac{3}{20}$		
2	$\frac{6}{20}$		
3	$\frac{9}{20}$		
4	$\frac{10}{20}$		
5	$\frac{19}{20}$		
	$\frac{1}{25}$	0.04	$\frac{1}{25}$ is equivalent to $\frac{4}{100}$ so $\frac{1}{25} = 0.04$
6	$\frac{3}{25}$		
7	$\frac{6}{25}$		
8	$\frac{10}{25}$		
9	$\frac{18}{25}$		

Stretch zone

True or false? 0.3 is less than $\frac{1}{2}$. _____

Explain your answer. _____

_____

_____

3H Place value in decimals

Discover   Student Book 6, page 73

- colouring pencils: red, blue, orange, yellow, purple, green, pink

This chart is named after Caleb Gattegno, a famous mathematics teacher.

This is called a Gattegno chart.

Thousands	1000	2000	3000	4000	5000	6000	7000	8000	9000
Hundreds	100	200	300	400	500	600	700	800	900
Tens	10	20	30	40	50	60	70	80	90
Ones	1	2	3	4	5	6	7	8	9
Tenths	0.1	0.2	0.3	0.4	0.5	0.6	0.7	0.8	0.9
Hundredths	0.01	0.02	0.03	0.04	0.05	0.06	0.07	0.08	0.09
Thousandths	0.001	0.002	0.003	0.004	0.005	0.006	0.007	0.008	0.009

Draw coloured dots on the chart to show these numbers.

The first one is done for you.

	grey	7.263	**4**	yellow	3726.5
1	red	26.154	**5**	purple	333.333
2	blue	37.265	**6**	green	892.870
3	orange	372.650	**7**	pink	89.287

Stretch zone

Describe three patterns you can see in the Gattegno chart.

1 _____

_____

2 _____

_____

3 _____

_____

Explore
Student Book 6, page 74

Solve these multiplications.

Use the place-value grids to help you.

The first one is done for you.

H = hundreds	t = tenths
T = tens	h = hundredths
O = ones	th = thousandths

5.327×100

H	T	O	.	t	h	th
		5	.	3	2	7
5	3	2	.	7		

$5.327 \times 100 =$

532.7

1 53.27×10

			.			
			.			

$53.27 \times 10 =$

2 85.721×10

			.			
			.			

$85.721 \times 10 =$

3 95.721×10

			.			
			.			

$95.721 \times 10 =$

4 0.123×100

			.			
			.			

$0.123 \times 100 =$

5 12.3×10

			.			
			.			

$0.123 \times 100 =$

Stretch zone

I multiply a number by 100. The answer is 10.

What number did I start with?

31 Multiplying decimals

Discover   Student Book 6, page 75

Draw place-value counters in the grids to solve these multiplications. One is done for you.

3.212 × 3 = [9.636]

Tens	Ones	•	Tenths	Hundredths	Thousandths
	(1) (1) (1)	.	(0.1) (0.1)	(0.01)	(0.001) (0.001)
	(1) (1) (1)	.	(0.1) (0.1)	(0.01)	(0.001) (0.001)
	(1) (1) (1)	.	(0.1) (0.1)	(0.01)	(0.001) (0.001)

1   1.242 × 2 = [   ]

Tens	Ones	•	Tenths	Hundredths	Thousandths
		.			
		.			

2   13.422 × 2 = [   ]

Tens	Ones	•	Tenths	Hundredths	Thousandths
		.			
		.			

3   13.113 × 3 = [   ]

Tens	Ones	•	Tenths	Hundredths	Thousandths
		.			
		.			
		.			

Stretch zone

Draw a place-value grid to calculate 7.35 × 3. You will need to exchange some counters.

Explore   Student Book 6, page 76

Estimate the answers to these multiplications. Then solve them using a written method.

The first one is done for you.

4.89 × 8

Estimate: 5 × 8 = 40

	4	.	8	9
×				8
	0	.	7	2
	6	.	4	0
3	2	.	0	0
3	9	.	1	2
			1	

(8 × 0.09)
(8 × 0.8)
(8 × 4)

1 2.45 × 3

Estimate: _____

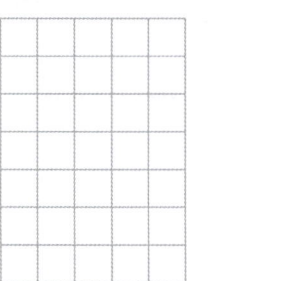

2 5 × 1.75

Estimate: _____

3 3 × 5.85

Estimate: _____

4 5.85 × 6

Estimate: _____

5 3.19 × 4

Estimate: _____

Stretch zone

Which of these multiplications do you think will have the greater product?

4.23 × 5   or   5.32 × 4

Solve each multiplication to check.

3J Dividing decimals

Discover
Student Book 6, page 77

Draw place-value counters in the grids to solve these divisions. One is done for you.

$6.336 \div 3 =$ | 2.112

Tens	Ones	•	Tenths	Hundredths	Thousandths
	(1)(1)	.	(0.1)	(0.01)	(0.001)(0.001)
	(1)(1)	.	(0.1)	(0.01)	(0.001)(0.001)
	(1)(1)	.	(0.1)	(0.01)	(0.001)(0.001)

1 $8.448 \div 2 =$

Tens	Ones	•	Tenths	Hundredths	Thousandths
		.			
		.			

2 $3.963 \div 3 =$

Tens	Ones	•	Tenths	Hundredths	Thousandths
		.			
		.			
		.			

3 $12.669 \div 3 =$

Tens	Ones	•	Tenths	Hundredths	Thousandths
		.			
		.			
		.			

Stretch zone

Solve **question 3** using the short division method.

3J Dividing decimals

Explore   Student Book 6, page 78

Estimate the answers to these divisions.

Then solve them using the short division method.

The first one is done for you.

$12.72 \div 6$

Estimate: $\underline{12 \div 6 = 2}$

		2	.	1	2	
6	1	2	.	7	¹2	

1 $12.72 \div 3$

Estimate: _____

2 $12.72 \div 2$

Estimate: _____

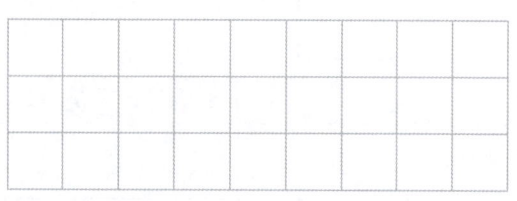

3 $12.72 \div 4$

Estimate: _____

4 $35.925 \div 5$

Estimate: _____

5 $25.44 \div 6$

Estimate: _____

6 $25.44 \div 3$

Estimate: _____

Stretch zone

What do you notice about the answers to **questions 5** and **6**?

Explain why this happens.

3K Decimal problems

Discover   Student Book 6, page 79

Here is a list of the reaction times of 6 athletes.

Round the reaction times to the specified degree of accuracy.

> The reaction time is the time from when the start gun is fired to the time the athlete starts running.

	Athlete	Reaction time (seconds)	Rounded to the nearest hundredth	Rounded to the nearest tenth	Rounded to the nearest second
1	Grace	0.243			
2	Sobia	0.476			
3	Zara	0.673			
4	Rowan	0.336			
5	Cam	0.824			
6	Hana	0.505			

7 List the athletes in order of reaction time, fastest to slowest.

Write each athlete's initial, instead of their full name.

a Use the actual times.   _____

b Use the times rounded to the nearest hundredth.   _____

c Use the times rounded to the nearest tenth.   _____

d Use the times rounded to the nearest second.   _____

8 What is the same and what is different about your answers for **question 7**?

_____

_____

9 What is the difference between the fastest and slowest reaction times?

a Use the actual times.   seconds

b Use the times rounded to the nearest hundredth.   seconds

Stretch zone

Write a sentence explaining the difference that rounding numbers makes to calculations.

Explore   Student Book 6, page 80

Here the annual profits of five companies.

Rewrite each amount in the form '£x.xx million'.

The first one is done for you.

Company	A	B	C	D	E
Profit in £	2 361 525	3 652 590	2 587 325	4 143 565	1 999 250
1 Profit written as '£x.xx million'	£2.36 million				

2 Write the companies in order of profit, from smallest to largest. _____

Use the rounded figures to calculate:

3 the difference in profit between the company that made most profit and the company that made least profit

£ [   ] million

4 the total profit for all five companies

£ [   ] million

5 Company C trebles its profit the following year.

What is the profit in that year?

£ [   ] million

6 Company D splits its profit equally between 5 investors.

How much does each investor receive?

£ [   ] million

Stretch zone

Calculate the total profit for all five companies.
Use the actual figures.

£ [   ]

Write this number in the form '£x.xx million'.

£ [   ] million

Is the answer the same as the answer for **question 4**? _____

3L Fractions, decimals and percentages

Discover   Student Book 6, page 81

Write these percentages as fractions.

Remember:

percentage means 'out of 100'.

1   25% = ☐

2   75% = ☐

3   10% = ☐

4   40% = ☐

5   20% = ☐

6   90% = ☐

7   50% = ☐

8   33.3̇% = ☐

9   66.6̇% = ☐

10   70% = ☐

Write the equivalent percentage for each test score.

Two are done for you.

Score (out of 60)	Equivalent %
60	100%
11 54	
12 45	
13 42	
14 30	

Score (out of 60)	Equivalent %
6	10%
15 15	
16 12	
17 24	
18 3	

Stretch zone

I have to get more than $\frac{7}{10}$ of the marks in a test to achieve an A grade.

The maximum score is 75.

What is the lowest score I could get and still get an A?   ☐

Explore Student Book 6, pages 82–83

Complete each diagram by writing six different percentages, fractions or decimals of the number in the middle.

Two are done for you.

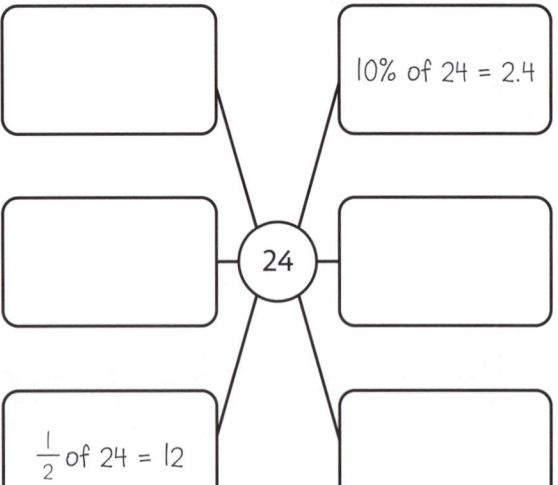

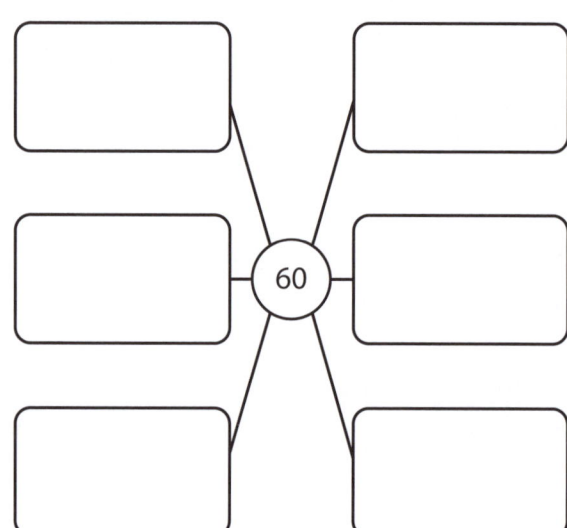

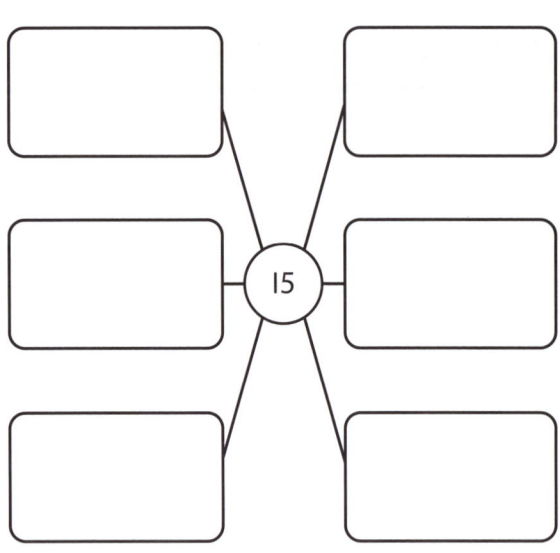

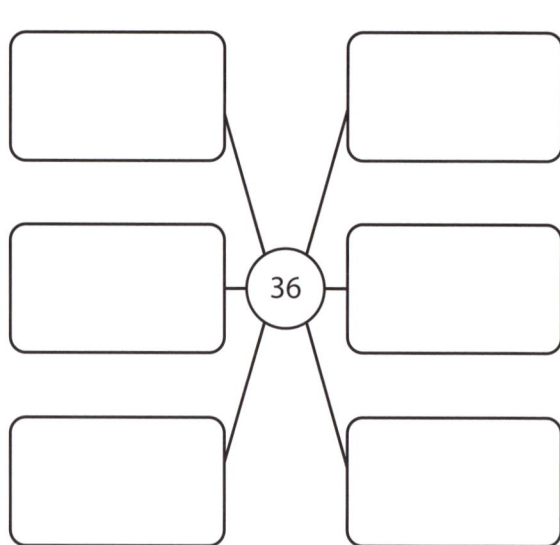

Stretch zone

Draw a diagram like this with 0.75 in the centre.

3 Fractions, decimals and percentages

Review

1 Draw a face next to each bubble to show how confident you feel about your learning.

comparing and ordering fractions, including fractions > 1

equivalent fractions, decimals and percentages

calculating with fractions

calculating with decimals

solving fraction and decimal problems

2 Tell a partner about one thing you did really well in this unit.

3 Write about what you found easy, what challenged you or what you found really hard.

What work did you feel really confident doing?

_____

_____

_____

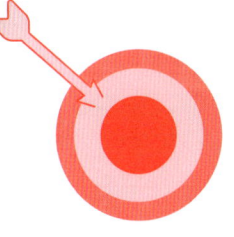

What work really stretched and challenged you?

_____

_____

_____

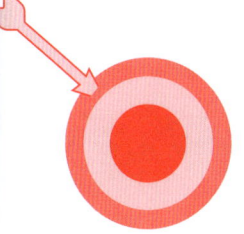

Is there any work you might need some extra help with?

_____

_____

4A Ratio

Discover

Student Book 6, page 87

What is the ratio of cracked eggs to uncracked eggs?

Draw a diagram to match each problem.

The first one is done for you.

> Remember:
>
> ratio compares **part** to **part**.

	Eggs in box	Cracked eggs	Ratio (cracked : uncracked)	Ratio (simplest terms)	Diagram
	25	15	15 : 10	3 : 2	
1	12	4			
2	16	2			
3	24	6			
4	15	3			
5	20	15			
6	15	12			

 **Stretch zone**

 Draw a diagram to show a ratio of 7 : 2.

4A Ratio

- colouring pencils: red and blue

Look at the pattern of floor tiles in room I.

Colour the tiles (B = blue, R = red).

Then answer the questions.

5 metres

B	R	B	R	B
R	B	R	B	R
B	R	B	R	B

3 metres

Room I

I   What is the ratio of blue tiles to red tiles in room I?

☐ : ☐

2   Room 2 is twice the length and twice the width of room I. It has the same tiling pattern.

What is the ratio of blue tiles to red tiles in room 2?

☐ : ☐

3   How many red tiles are there in room 2?

☐ red tiles

4   Room 3 is 2 tiles longer and 2 tiles wider than room 2. It has the same tiling pattern.

What is the ratio of blue tiles to red tiles in room 3?

☐ : ☐

5   Draw a pattern with tiles in the ratio 2 : 3.

Stretch zone

Look again at the pattern for room I. True or false?
Every time I add a row of tiles, the ratio of blue to red stays the same.
Explain your answer.

4B Proportion

Discover
Student Book 6, page 89

Write the proportion of each grid that is shaded.

Write the proportion as a fraction, a decimal and a percentage.

The first one is done for you.

> Remember:
>
> proportion compares a **part** to the **whole**.

Grid	Proportion that is shaded		
	Fraction	Decimal	Percentage
	$\frac{3}{10}$	0.3	30%
1			
2			
3			
4			
5			

Shade these grids to match the proportions shown.

6   0.75 or 75% shaded

7   0.125 or 12.5% shaded

Stretch zone

Draw a bar model to show a proportion of 0.625.

Use the smallest number of divisions you can.

4B Proportion

- a newspaper

Complete this table by calculating the proportion of each type of content in a newspaper.

Write the fractions in their simplest forms.

First you need to calculate the total number of pages.

The first column is done for you.

The contents of a daily newspaper by number of pages

Content	World news	National news	Local news	Politics	Business	Sport	Other
Number of pages	10	15	8	5	4	6	2
Proportion (fraction)	$\frac{1}{5}$						
Proportion (%)	20%						

Look at a real newspaper.

Record the number of pages in this table.

Calculate the proportion of each type of content.

Content	World news	National news	Local news	Politics	Business	Sport	Other
Number of pages							
Proportion (fraction)							
Proportion (%)							

Stretch zone

You are editing a newspaper for school. Draw a table to show the proportions of different types of content you will include.

4C Percentage problems

Discover
Student Book 6, page 91

Complete this table.

Round the amounts to the nearest cent if necessary.

The first column is done for you.

> You may need to write some workings on scrap paper.

Items for the school snack stall: cost prices and profits

Item	Mango	Banana	Bag of nuts	Oat bar	Juice carton
Cost price	$1.05	$0.33	$1.50	$0.60	$0.75
10% profit margin	$0.11				
15% profit margin	$0.16				
$33\frac{1}{3}$% profit margin	$0.35				

Decide how much you would sell each item for.

You do not have to make the same profit on each item.

> If possible, discuss and agree your sale prices with a partner.

Item	Sale price	Reason
Mango		
Banana		
Bag of nuts		
Oat bar		
Juice carton		

Stretch zone

True or false? In a sale, I reduce all the prices by 50%. If I reduce the prices by 50% again, everything will be free. Explain your answer.

_____

_____

_____

4C Percentage problems

Student Book 6, page 92

Explore

	Full price
Monthly fee	$25
Swim (I hour)	$8.50
Gym (I hour)	$7.50
Fitness class (30 minutes)	$15
Personal trainer (2 hours)	$35

TC Fitness — This month only

Monthly fee	25% off!
Swimming	10% off!
Gym	10% off!
Personal training	half price!

A new fitness club opens. For the first month, there are some special offers.

Solve these problems. Show your workings.

1 Zahid visits three times this month. For each visit, he spends I hour swimming and I hour in the fitness room. What is the total cost?

$

2 Emma visits four times this month. For three of her visits, she spends I hour swimming and 2 hours in the gym. For her fourth visit, she spends 2 hours with a personal trainer and does a 30-minute fitness class. What is the total cost?

$

3 Lu visits twice this month. For his first visit, he tries everything. For his second visit, he only goes to the gym, for 2 hours. What is the total cost?

$

4 Piper visits 4 times this month. For every visit, she spends I hour swimming and I hour in the gym, followed by two 30-minute fitness classes. What is the total cost?

$

Stretch zone

You can visit the gym four times this month. You have a $100 budget. How will you spend it?

4 Ratio and proportion

83

4D Scaling problems

Discover   Student Book 6, page 93

- a ruler

Scale factor 3 means '3 times the size'.

Draw these shapes on the grid. For each pair, draw the shapes inside each other. Draw:

1 an isosceles triangle with base 1.5 cm, and its enlargement by scale factor 3

2 a square with sides 2.5 cm, and its enlargement by scale factor 2

3 a right-angled triangle with sides 3, 4 and 5 cm, and a similar triangle half its size.

Stretch zone

Draw a shape of your own on the grid. Then enlarge it by scale factor 1.5.

4D Scaling problems

Explore   Student Book 6, page 94

- A3 paper (297 × 420 mm)
- a ruler

You are going to draw a scale drawing of the solar system to fit on a sheet of A3 paper (420 mm x 297 mm).

Decide on an appropriate design and scale to use.

Use this space for your workings and a rough sketch.

Planet	Average distance from Sun (million km)
Mercury	58
Venus	110
Earth	150
Mars	230
Jupiter	780
Saturn	1430
Uranus	2900
Neptune	4500

Scale: _____

 Now draw your scale drawing on a sheet of A3 paper. Do not forget to include the scale.

Stretch zone

On a large sheet of paper, draw a scale drawing of your home.
(Or you could just do a single room if you like.)

4 Ratio and proportion

Review

1   Draw a face next to each bubble to show how confident you feel about your learning.

solving problems about ratio and proportion

solving problems using percentages

using scale factors when drawing

solving problems involving unequal sharing and grouping

2   Tell a partner about one thing you did really well in this unit.

3   Write about what you found easy, what challenged you or what you found really hard.

What work did you feel really confident doing?

_____

_____

_____

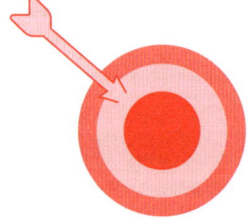

What work really stretched and challenged you?

_____

_____

_____

_____

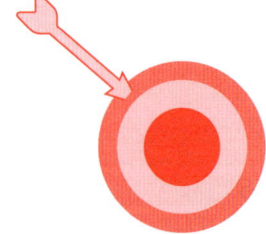

Is there any work you might need some extra help with?

_____

_____

5A Number sequences

Discover
Student Book 6, page 98

Create number sequences by calculating the perimeters of the rectangles.

1

Dimensions of rectangle	1 × 2	1 × 3	1 × 4	1 × 5	1 × 6
Perimeter of rectangle					

2

Dimensions of rectangle	2 × 2	2 × 3	2 × 4	2 × 5	2 × 6
Perimeter of rectangle					

3

Dimensions of rectangle	3 × 2	3 × 3	3 × 4	3 × 5	3 × 6
Perimeter of rectangle					

4

Dimensions of rectangle	4 × 2	4 × 3	4 × 4	4 × 5	4 × 6
Perimeter of rectangle					

5

Dimensions of rectangle	5 × 2	5 × 3	5 × 4	5 × 5	5 × 6
Perimeter of rectangle					

Stretch zone

Can you predict the rule for this sequence without calculating the perimeters?

_____

_____

Dimensions of rectangle	6 × 2	6 × 3	6 × 4	6 × 5	6 × 6
Perimeter of rectangle					

5A Number sequences

Explore Student Book 6, pages 99–100

Follow these steps five times to make your own number sequences.

- Choose a start number.
- Make up a rule: an operation (+ or −) and a number.
- Write the first eight terms of the sequence.
- An example is shown in the table.

Write something you notice about each sequence.

A **term** is a number in a sequence.

Look at this sequence:

5, 11, 17, 23, 29, 35, …

The first term is 5, the fourth term is 23 and the sixth term is 35.

Start number	Rule	Sequence							
15	⁻7	15	8	1	⁻6	⁻13	⁻20	⁻27	⁻34

I notice that: the first three numbers are positive. The others are negative.

| | | | | | | | |

I notice that:

| | | | | | | | |

I notice that:

| | | | | | | | |

I notice that:

| | | | | | | | |

I notice that:

| | | | | | | | |

I notice that:

Stretch zone

Create a number sequence. The first term must be 2. The fifth term must be 30. Write the rule.

| 2 | | | | 30 |

Rule: _____

5B Using a formula

Discover
Student Book 6, page 101

The formula for the area of a triangle is $\frac{1}{2}$ (**base × height**).

Use the formula to calculate the areas of these triangles.

The first two areas are done for you.

What do you notice about each sequence of areas?

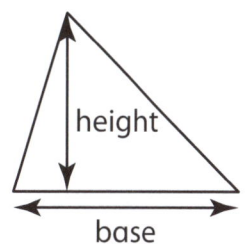

height

base

1

	Triangle I	Triangle 2	Triangle 3	Triangle 4	Triangle 5
Base	2 cm	3 cm	4 cm	5 cm	6 cm
Height	2 cm	2 cm	2 cm	2 cm	2 cm
Area	2 cm²	3 cm²			

I notice that: _____

2

	Triangle I	Triangle 2	Triangle 3	Triangle 4	Triangle 5
Base	2 cm	3 cm	4 cm	5 cm	6 cm
Height	3 cm	3 cm	3 cm	3 cm	3 cm
Area					

I notice that: _____

3

	Triangle I	Triangle 2	Triangle 3	Triangle 4	Triangle 5
Base	2 cm	3 cm	4 cm	5 cm	6 cm
Height	4 cm	4 cm	4 cm	4 cm	4 cm
Area					

I notice that: _____

 **Stretch zone**

 Create a spreadsheet on the computer. Use a formula to calculate the areas.

5B Using a formula

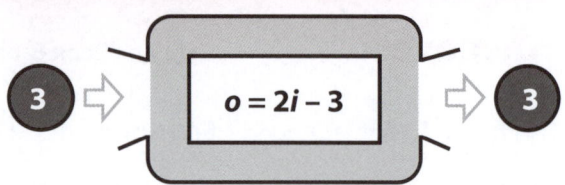

The formula for this function machine is **o = 2i − 3**.

If *i* = 3, *o* is also 3.

Look at the rule for each function machine.

Write the output for each number.

The first one is done for you.

i = input number and *o* = output number.

1

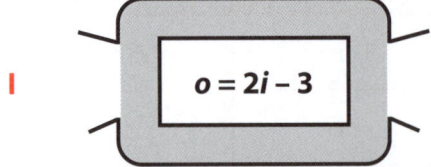

$o = 2i - 3$

Input	3	4	5	6	7	8
Output	3					

2

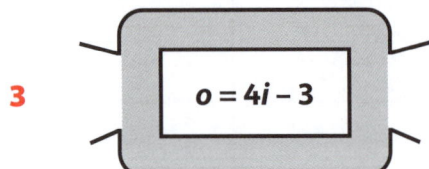

$o = 3i - 3$

Input	3	4	5	6	7	8
Output						

3

$o = 4i - 3$

Input	3	4	5	6	7	8
Output						

4

$o = 5i - 3$

Input	3	4	5	6	7	8
Output						

Stretch zone

How could you predict the outputs for machine **4**, using the outputs for machine **3**?

_____

_____

_____

5C Missing number problems

Discover   Student Book 6, page 103

Work out the missing values.

		Value
1	⬤ ⬤ ⬤ ⬤	
	⬛ ⬛ ⬛	12
2	⬛ ▲	
	▲ ⬤ ⬤	11
	⬤ ▲ ⬛	12

Work out the value of these.

		Value
3	⬤	
4	⬛	
5	▲	

		Value
6	⬤ + ▲	
7	▲ − ⬤	
8	2 × ⬛ − ▲	

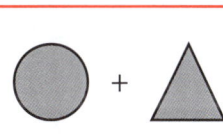

Stretch zone

Make up your own puzzle like this for a partner to solve.

Check their answers.

Explore
Student Book 6, page 104

Jada is given $75 for her birthday. She then gets $10 allowance each week.

We can calculate her total using this equation: **75 + 10w** (*w* stands for 'weeks')

To work out how much Jada has after 5 weeks, I substitute 5 for *w*:

$75 + (10 \times 5) = 75 + 50 = \$125$

Use the equation to calculate how much Jada has after these numbers of weeks.

1 10 weeks   **2** 15 weeks   **3** 20 weeks

4 Write an equation for this statement:

Tam starts with $45 and then gets $15 a week. _____

Use the equation to calculate how much Tam has after these numbers of weeks.

5 1 week   **6** 5 weeks   **7** 10 weeks

8 Write an equation for this statement:

Ali knocks downs a wall in his back yard. It is 12 m long.
He knocks down a 1.5 m wide section per day. What length of the wall is still standing?

_____

Use the equation to calculate how high the wall is after these numbers of days.

9 1 day   **10** 3 days   **11** 6 days

12 How many days will it take Ali to knock the whole wall down? _____

Stretch zone

Why is the answer to **question 3** not twice the answer to **question 1**, even though Jada has saved up for twice the length of time?

5D Problems with two unknowns

Discover
Student Book 6, page 105

I go to a zoo. In the insect house I see some spiders and beetles.

I can see 14 bodies and 100 legs.

How many spiders and how many beetles are there?

Show all your workings.

There are [   ] spiders and [   ] beetles.

Stretch zone

Make up a similar problem about starfishes and octopuses.

Ask a partner to solve it. Check their answer.

_____

_____

_____

_____

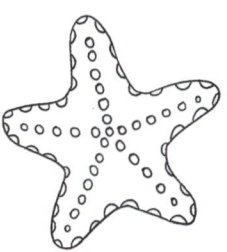

5D Problems with two unknowns

Explore   Student Book 6, page 106

Write an equation for each number puzzle. Find all the possible solutions.

The first one is done for you.

I am thinking of two whole numbers. I add them together. The answer is 12.

Equation: $\underline{\text{x + y = 12}}$

Solutions: $\underline{0 + 12,\ 1 + 11,\ 2 + 10,\ 3 + 9,\ 4 + 8,\ 5 + 7,\ 6 + 6}$

1 I am thinking of two whole numbers. I double the first one, then add the second. The answer is 15.

Equation: _____

Solutions: _____

2 I am thinking of two whole numbers. I halve the first one, then add the second. The answer is 15.

Equation: _____

Solutions: _____

3 I am thinking of two whole numbers. I double each of them, then add the totals together. The answer is 16.

Equation: _____

Solutions: _____

4 I am thinking of two whole numbers. I add them together, then double the total. The answer is 16.

Equation: _____

Solutions: _____

Stretch zone

In **questions 3** and **4**, both puzzles involve adding and doubling, and the answer is 16.

What is the same and what is different about the equations and the solutions?

5E Variables

Discover   Student Book 6, page 107

Complete these tables for the given equations.

The first one is done for you.

$y = 3x - 4$

Value of x	1	2	3	4	5
Value of y	⁻1	2	5	8	11

These equations are similar to the function machines on page 90.

Here the 'input' is called x and the 'output' is called y.

$y = 3x - 4$ is the same as a function machine that looks like this:

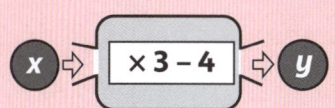

1 $y = 3x - 5$

Value of x	1	2	3	4	5
Value of y					

2 $y = 3x - 6$

Value of x	1	2	3	4	5
Value of y					

3 $y = 2x - 4$

Value of x	1	2	3	4	5
Value of y					

4 $y = 2x - 5$

Value of x	1	2	3	4	5
Value of y					

5 $y = 4x - 4$

Value of x	1	2	3	4	5
Value of y					

Stretch zone

What is the 'common difference' for each table? For the example table, the common difference is 3, as the value of y increases by 3 each time.

$y = 3x - 4$: [3] $y = 3x - 5$: [   ] $y = 3x - 6$: [   ]

$y = 2x - 4$: [   ] $y = 2x - 5$: [   ] $y = 4x - 4$: [   ]

5E Variables

Explore   Student Book 6, page 108

Solve these equations. Show your workings.

Check your answers by substituting the solution for the number.

The first one is done for you.

Equation	Workings	Solution	Check by substituting
$2c - 4 = 22$	$2c = 22 + 4 = 26$ $26 \div 2 = 13$	$c = 13$	$(2 \times \underline{13}) - 4 = 22$
1 $3a - 5 = 22$			
2 $4b + 2 = 18$			
3 $4c + 3 = 19$			
4 $5d - 20 = 15$			
5 $5e + 5 = 20$			
6 $6.5f - 6 = 20$			

Stretch zone

Write an equation where n is equal to 7.

_____

5 Algebra

Review

1 Draw a face next to each bubble to show how confident you feel about your learning.

finding rules for number sequences ◯

using simple formulae ◯

solving missing number problems ◯

solving problems with two unknowns ◯

2 Tell a partner about one thing you did really well in this unit.

3 Write about what you found easy, what challenged you or what you found really hard.

What work did you feel really confident doing?

_____

_____

_____

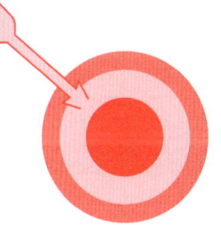

What work really stretched and challenged you?

_____

_____

_____

_____

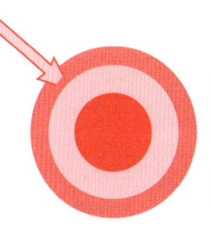

Is there any work you might need some extra help with?

_____

_____

6A Comparing units of measure

Discover
Student Book 6, page 112

- measuring equipment: ruler, tape measure, weighing scales, measuring containers
- Internet access for checking distance in kilometres (km)

Follow these steps for each unit of measurement below.

- Find something that you would measure using the given unit.
- Find the actual measurement and record it in the table.

You do not need to fill in the grey cells.

- Convert the measurement to the other units shown.

The first one is done for you.

Length/distance

Unit	Thing to measure	mm	cm	m	km
millimetres	width of pencil	5	0.5	0.005	
centimetres					
metres					
kilometres					

Mass

Unit	Thing to measure	mg	g	kg
milligrams				
grams				
kilograms				

Capacity

Unit	Thing to measure	ml	ℓ
millilitres			
litres			

Stretch zone

Find a light object. What is it? _____ Weigh it.

Write the mass in grams. Convert it to kilograms. ⬚ g = ⬚ kg

6A Comparing units of measure

Solve these problems. Show your workings.

1 A bottle of water holds 335 ml. There are 30 people in my class.
They drink a bottle each. How much water do they drink altogether?

 litres

2 You are packing for a holiday. The weight limit is 18 kg. You pack a laptop
(4.55 kg), three books (375 g each) and clothes (9.55 kg). Your suitcase
weighs 3.8 kg.

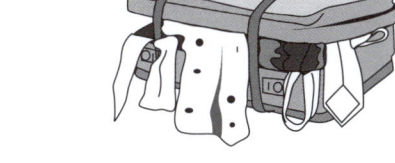

a How much does everything weigh in total?

 kilograms

b How much of your weight limit do you have left?

 kilograms

3 I am going to post a package. There are five items in the package. They weigh
250 g, 350 g, 1.65 kg, 1500 g and 1.25 kg. The postage is $1.50 for every 500 g.
How much does it cost to post the parcel?

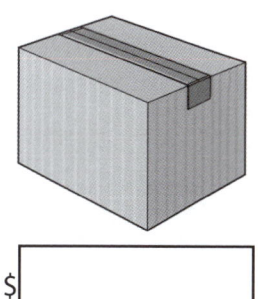

$

Stretch zone

Make up your own word problem based on mass. The answer must be 1.755 kg.

6 Length, mass and capacity

6B Converting units of measure

Discover

Student Book 6, pages 115–116

Complete the conversion table.

	Conversion table		
1	1 km	=	m
2	1 m	=	cm
3	1 cm	=	mm
4	1 ℓ	=	cl
5	1 ℓ	=	ml
6	1 cl	=	ml
7	1 kg	=	g
8	1 g	=	mg

Work out these conversions.

9 8.7 km = ☐ m

10 8.75 m = ☐ cm

11 89.5 cm = ☐ mm

12 5.55 ℓ = ☐ cl

13 8.45 cl = ☐ ml

14 8.95 kg = ☐ g

15 9.65 g = ☐ mg

16 5500 m = ☐ km

17 9850 ml = ☐ ℓ

18 6750 g = ☐ kg

19 1.575 ℓ = ☐ ml

20 2550 mm = ☐ m

Stretch zone

How do the names of the units help you remember the conversion rules?

_____

_____

_____

_____

_____

_____

6B Converting units of measure

Explore
Student Book 6, pages 117–118

- a calculator
- a map or an atlas

Solve these problems. Show your workings.

1 If you walk 1 million metres from your home where will you be?

You can choose which direction to walk in.

_____

2 Jaden sells bottles of juice. A bottle holds 240 ml. He has 21.75 ℓ of juice.
How many bottles can he fill?

3 One grain of sand weighs 0.05 mg.
What is the mass of 1 000 000 grains of sand?

Give your answer in grams.

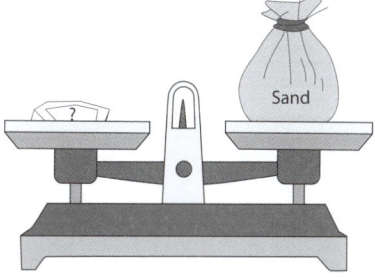

☐ grams

Stretch zone

In each breath, you breathe about 500 ml of air.

Estimate how much air you breathe in a week.
Show your workings.

☐ litres

6C Reading scales and measuring accurately

Discover
Student Book 6, page 119

- a ruler
- weighing scales ('Stretch zone' only)

You are going to design a pencil case to hold all your pens, pencils and other school equipment.

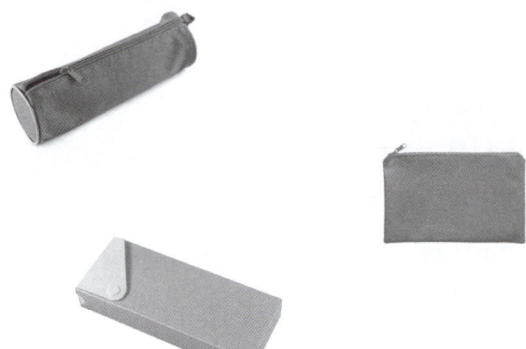

Answer these questions to help you design a pencil case that is just right for you.

1 What is your longest pen, pencil or other piece of equipment?

Measure it to the nearest millimetre and record it in the table below.

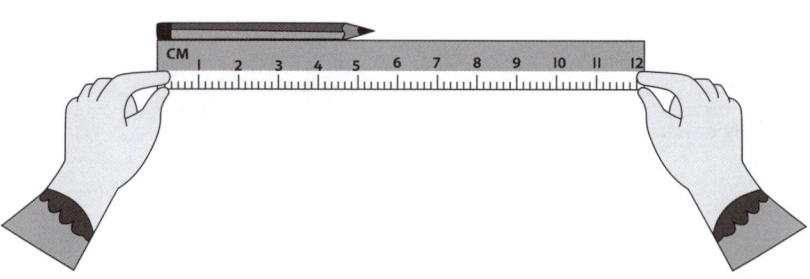

2 List some of your other items and their lengths in the table.

Item	Length (mm)

Item	Length (mm)

You will continue with your pencil case design on the next page.

Stretch zone

Hold all the items in your hand. Estimate their mass.

Estimate: [   ] g

Use scales to see how accurate your estimate was.

Actual mass: [   ] g

6C Reading scales and measuring accurately

Explore Student Book 6, pages 120–121

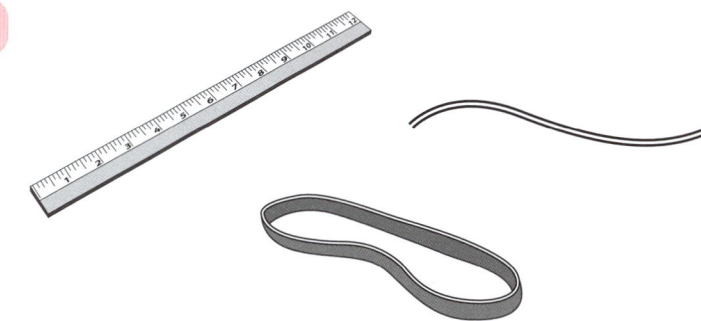

- a ruler
- an elastic band
- a piece of string

On this page, you will continue to work on your pencil case design.

1 Gather all your pens, pencils and other equipment into a bundle.

Hold them together with an elastic band.

Measure the length, width and depth that the pencil case will need to be to hold them all.

Measure to the nearest 0.5 cm.

Length: [ ] cm   Width: [ ] cm   Depth: [ ] cm

2 Use a piece of string to measure the distance around the bundle of equipment.

Then use a ruler to measure the string.

Measure to the nearest $\frac{1}{2}$ cm.

Distance around the equipment: [ ] cm

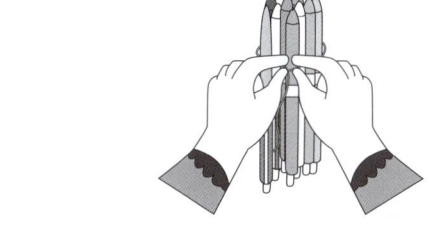

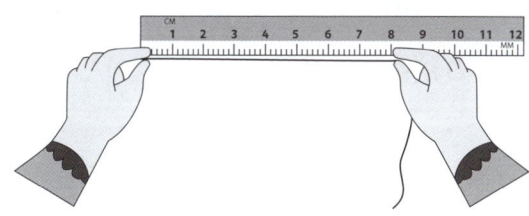

You now have all the dimensions you need for your pencil case.

3 Decide what shape you want your pencil case to be.

Do you want a cylinder, a cuboid, a triangular prism or another shape?

_____

Stretch zone

Draw a net for your pencil case. Label the sides with the dimensions.

Your sketch of the net does not have to be to scale.

6D Imperial units

Discover   Student Book 6, page 122

Complete these tables to convert from imperial units to metric units.

Most of these conversions are approximations.

1

Inches	1	10	20	50	100
Centimetres	2.54				

2

Yards	1	10	20	50	100
Metres	0.91				

3

Pints	1	10	20	50	100
Litres	0.57				

4

Pounds	1	10	20	50	100
Kilograms	0.45				

5

Ounces	1	10	20	50	100
Grams	28.35				

Stretch zone

Measure the length of this book.

Record it in centimetres, to 1 decimal place.

[   ] cm

Use the table in **question 1** to convert the length to inches. Show your workings.

Give your answer to the nearest half-inch.

[   ] inches

6D Imperial units

Explore Student Book 6, page 123

Complete this table to convert between miles and kilometres.

1

Miles	1	2	5	10	25	100
Kilometres			8			

Use the table to help you answer these questions. Show your workings.

2 I run a 10 km race. How far is this in miles?

☐ miles

3 I drive for 100 km. How far is this in miles?

☐ miles

4 I drive for 150 miles. How far is this in km?

☐ km

5 Hamad walks 20 miles. Marco walks 20 km. Who walks further? By how much?

_____ walks _____ further.

6 One lap of an athletics track is 400 m. I run 10 laps. How far did I run in miles?

☐ miles

Stretch zone

Aidan says: 'To convert miles to kilometres, you multiply by 5 and then divide by 8.'

Is he correct? _____ Explain your answer.

_____

_____

6 Length, mass and capacity

Review

1 Draw a face next to each bubble to show how confident you feel about your learning.

measuring length, mass and capacity accurately ⃝

converting between different metric units of measurement ⃝

converting between metric and imperial units ⃝

solving measurement problems ⃝

2 Tell a partner about one thing you did really well in this unit.

3 Write about what you found easy, what challenged you or what you found really hard.

What work did you feel really confident doing?

_____

_____

_____

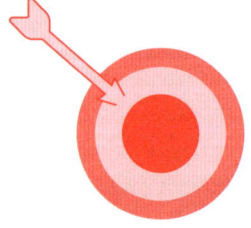

What work really stretched and challenged you?

_____

_____

_____

_____

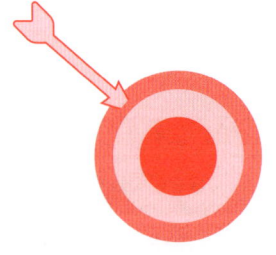

Is there any work you might need some extra help with?

_____

_____

7A Area and perimeter of rectilinear shapes

Discover
Student Book 6, page 127

You are going to design a school playground.

You have enough money to buy 40 square metres of a special surface that will make the playground safe to play in.

Draw three different designs for the playground that each have an area of 40 square metres.

I grid square = I square metre.

Stretch zone

What is the perimeter of each design? Write the perimeters on the grid.

If fencing costs £2.75 per metre, choose one design and calculate the cost of fencing.

Write the cost next to your chosen design.

Explore

Student Book 6, page 128

Draw rectilinear shapes that have these properties.

Label each shape with its letter:

A a perimeter of 20 cm

B an area of 18 cm^2

C a perimeter of 28 cm

D an area of 36 cm^2

E an area of 40 cm^2

F a perimeter of 32 cm

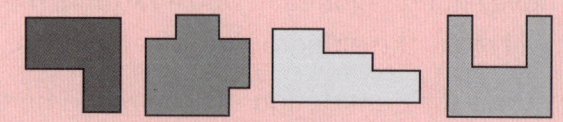

These are examples of rectilinear shapes.

I grid square = I square centimetre.

Stretch zone

Draw three rectilinear shapes with perimeter 20 cm. Which has the greatest area?

Discover

Student Book 6, pages 129–130

- a ruler

I grid square = I square centimetre.

Sketch three triangles, each with an area of 18 cm²: one right-angled, one isosceles, one scalene.

Label the base and perpendicular height for each triangle with its measurement.

Formula for the area of a triangle:

area = $\frac{1}{2}$(base × perpendicular height)

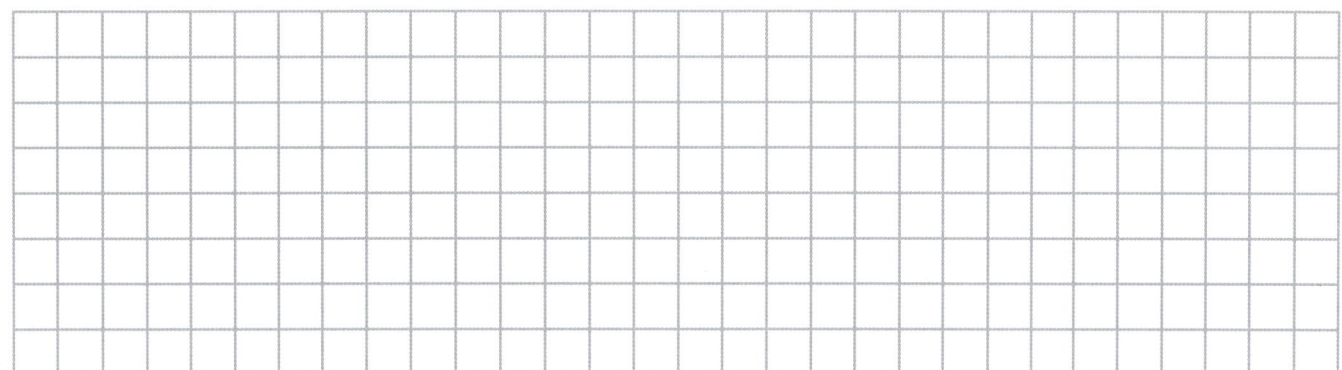

Sketch three parallelograms, each with an area of 36 cm².

Label the base and perpendicular height for each parallelogram.

Formula for the area of a parallelogram:

area = length × perpendicular height

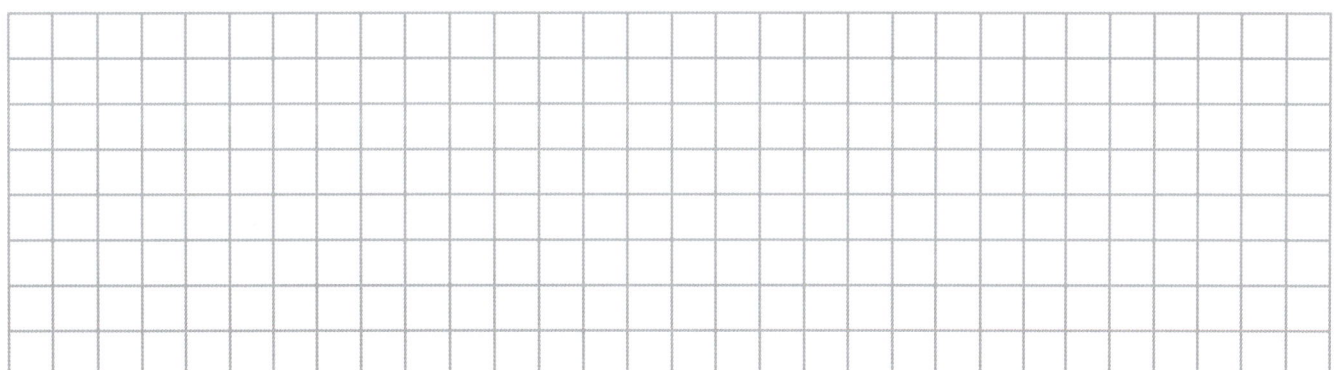

Stretch zone

Make a parallelogram by flipping one of the triangles that you drew. (You may need to draw this on squared paper.)

What is the area of your parallelogram?

This is an example of an isosceles triangle that has been flipped to make a parallelogram.

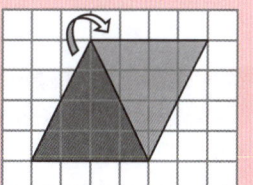

7 Area, perimeter and volume

Explore Student Book 6, page 131

Find the areas of these triangles and parallelograms.

1

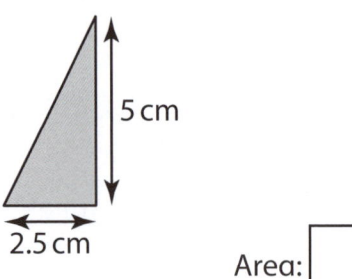

Area: ☐ cm²

2

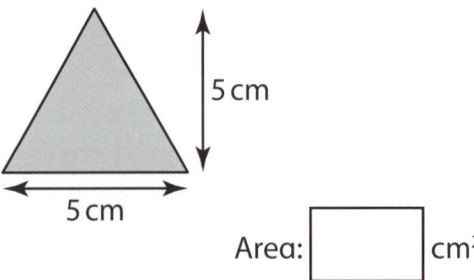

Area: ☐ cm²

3

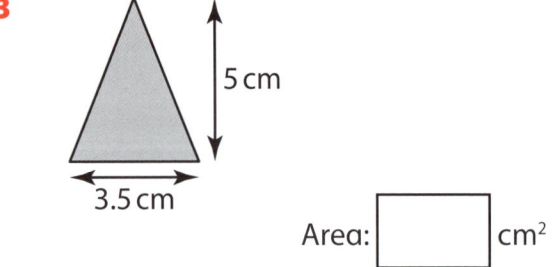

Area: ☐ cm²

4

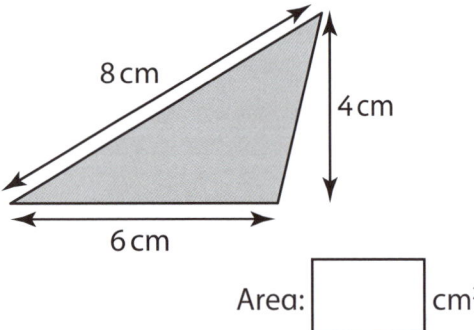

Area: ☐ cm²

5

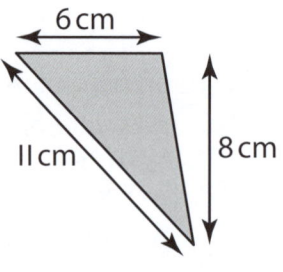

Area: ☐ cm²

6

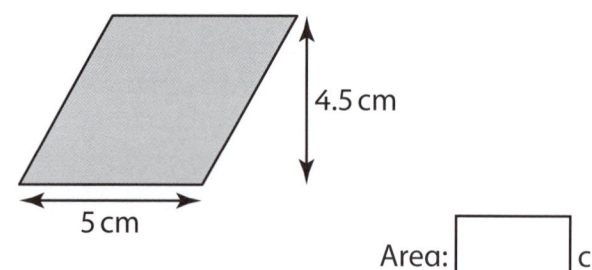

Area: ☐ cm²

7

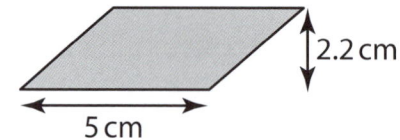

Area: ☐ cm²

8

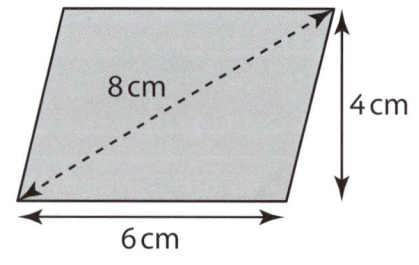

Area: ☐ cm²

Stretch zone

 What is the same and what is different about the shapes in **questions 4** and **8**?

Discover
Student Book 6, page 132

Draw four different shapes on the grid below.

Each shape must have an area of 24 cm².

None of your shapes can be a rectangle.

Consider composite shapes made up of rectangles, triangles and parallelograms.

I grid square = I square centimetre.

Stretch zone

On the grid above, draw a rectangle, a triangle and a parallelogram that each have the same area. Write the area inside each shape.

7C Calculating areas of irregular shapes

Explore   Student Book 6, page 133

Draw these composite shapes on the grid below.

Label each shape with its letter:

I grid square = I square centimetre.

A a shape made up of a square and an isosceles triangle, with an area of 30 cm²

B a shape made up of a rhombus and a right-angled triangle, with an area of 36 cm²

C a shape made up of a parallelogram and an isosceles triangle, with an area of 28 cm²

Stretch zone

On the grid above, draw a composite shape made up of a triangle, a rectangle and a parallelogram, with an area of 36 cm². Label this shape with the letter D.

7D Calculating volume

Discover
Student Book 6, page 134

Calculate the volumes of these six cuboids.

Formula for calculating the volume of a cuboid:

Volume = length × height × width

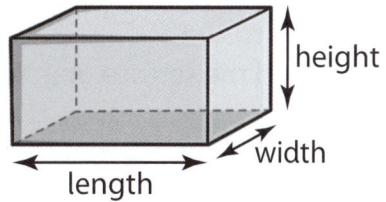

	Length (cm)	Width (cm)	Height (cm)	Volume (cm³)
1	6 cm	2 cm	2 cm	
2	6 cm	3 cm	3 cm	
3	6 cm	4 cm	4 cm	
4	6 cm	5 cm	5 cm	
5	6 cm	6 cm	6 cm	
6	6 cm	7 cm	7 cm	

7 What pattern do you see in the sequence of volumes?

_____

_____

_____

8 Explain why this pattern is formed.

_____

_____

_____

Stretch zone

True or false? If I double all the dimensions of a cuboid, the volume will also be doubled.

_____ Give examples to support your answer.

7D Calculating volume

Explore
Student Book 6, page 135

Sketch the net of the box on the grid below. It does not have to be to scale.

Work out the perimeter and the surface area (total area) of the net.

Calculate the volume of the box.

● a cardboard box

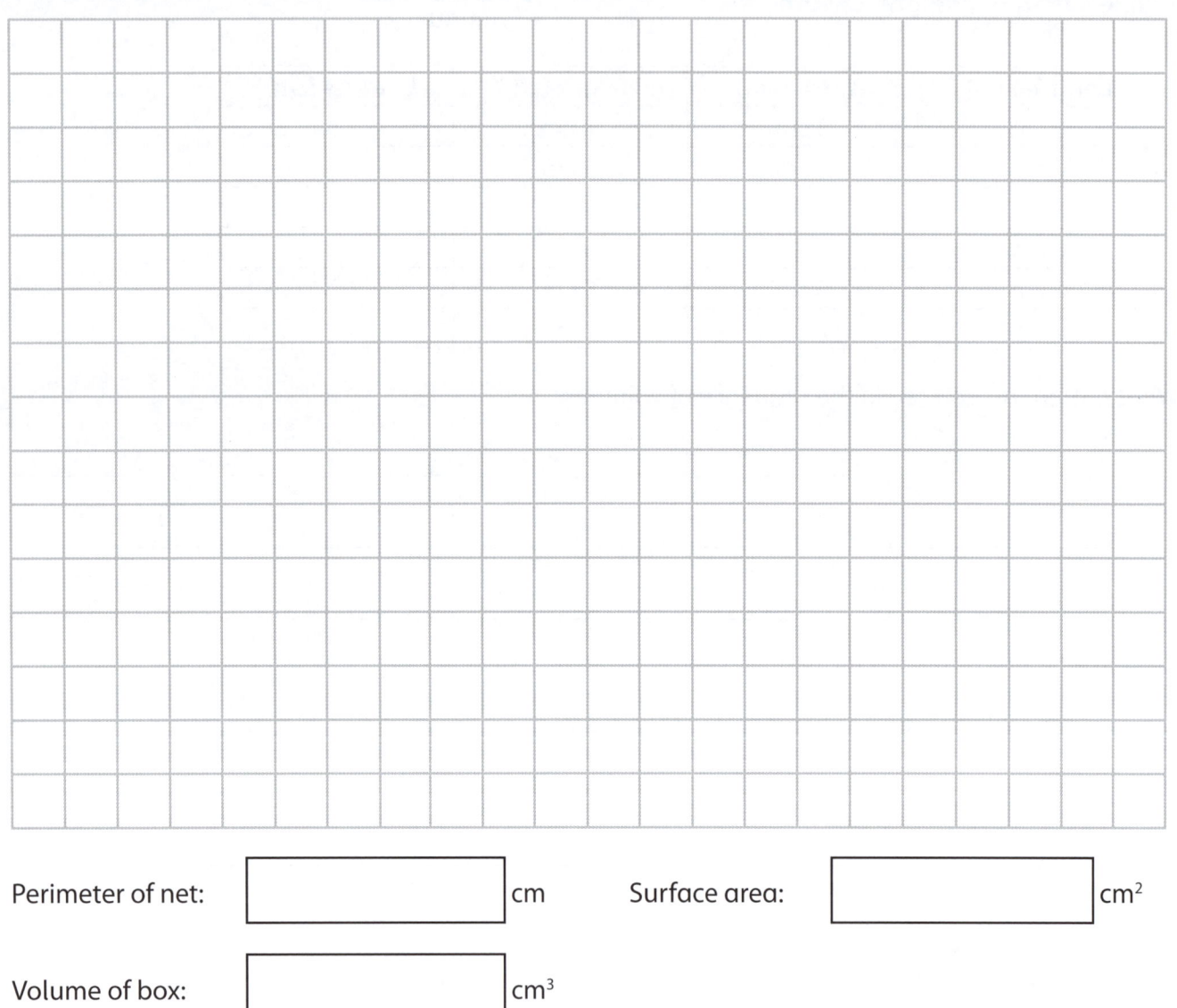

Perimeter of net: ☐ cm   Surface area: ☐ cm²

Volume of box: ☐ cm³

Stretch zone

How can you change the box so that it has half the volume of the original box?

_____

_____

_____

7 Area, perimeter and volume

Review

I Draw a face next to each bubble to show how confident you feel about your learning.

comparing areas and perimeters of shapes ◯

calculating areas of triangles and parallelograms ◯

calculating volumes of cuboids ◯

2 Tell a partner about one thing you did really well in this unit.

3 Write about what you found easy, what challenged you or what you found really hard.

What work did you feel really confident doing?

_____

_____

_____

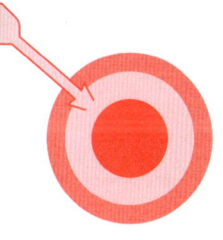

What work really stretched and challenged you?

_____

_____

_____

_____

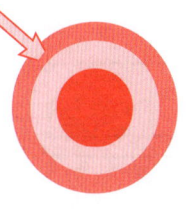

Is there any work you might need some extra help with?

_____

_____

8A Converting between units of time

Discover
Student Book 6, page 139

For each question, write the start time on the digital clock. Use 24-hour clock time.

Then calculate the end time. Show the end time on the analogue clock.

The first one is done for you.

	Start time	Duration	End time
	6 minutes to 9 in the morning	2 hours 13 minutes	
1	18 minutes past 11 in the morning	3 hours 28 minutes	
2	25 minutes to 5 in the afternoon	5 hours 35 minutes	
3	17 minutes past 10 in the evening	4 hours 28 minutes	
4	5 minutes to midnight	7 hours 39 minutes	

Stretch zone

Write three pairs of times that are 3 hours 25 minutes apart.

Write the times using the 24-hour clock.

[   ] and [   ]

[   ] and [   ]

[   ] and [   ]

8A Converting between units of time

Explore
Student Book 6, pages 140–141

- a calculator

Solve these problems. Show your workings.

1 I was born on 8 June 1959. How many days old am I?

	days

2 African elephants live for an average of 57 years in the wild and only 17 years in captivity. How many weeks longer do elephants in the wild live than elephants in captivity?

	weeks

3 Al-Khwarizmi wrote a famous mathematics book in the year 830. How many decades ago did he write the book?

	decades

4 What date will it be 1 million days after the start of this millennium?

_____

Stretch zone

How many milliseconds are you at school each day?

	milliseconds

8B Using the 24-hour clock and timetables

Use this grid to plan your ideal timetable for a week at school.

Write the days that you attend school in the top row.

Write the times of the lessons and breaks in the left-hand column. Use the 24-hour clock.

You can decide your own start and finish times.

Write five facts about your timetable.

_____

_____

_____

_____

_____

Stretch zone

If you could change one thing about your real school timetable, what would you change, and why?

8B Using the 24-hour clock and timetables

Explore

Student Book 6, page 143

Design a flight timetable from Dubai airport for one day (24 hours).

Rules

- There must be one flight to each destination.
- The first flight cannot leave before 06:30.
- The last flight must leave before 23:15.
- There must be at least half an hour between departure times.
- No flights are allowed to leave between 11 a.m. and 1 p.m.
- The Salalah flight must arrive in Salalah before 17:00.
- Spread departure times as evenly as possible throughout the day.

Durations of flights from Dubai airport

Abujah	7 hours 20 minutes
Amman	3 hours 10 minutes
Bangkok	6 hours 30 minutes
Cairo	3 hours 45 minutes
Salalah	1 hour 50 minutes
Jeddah	3 hours 2 minutes
Manchester	7 hours 35 minutes
Moscow	5 hours 20 minutes

Destination	Departure time	Arrival time (Dubai time)

Stretch zone

What do you think is the most important thing to consider when designing a timetable like this? Explain your answer.

8C Time zone problems

Discover   Student Book 6, page 144

These clocks show you the times in some cities around the world.

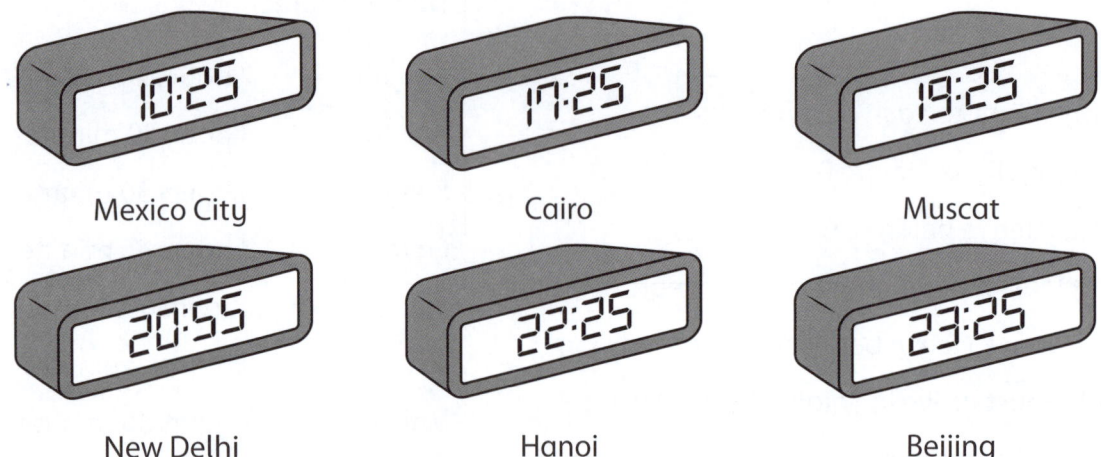

| Mexico City | Cairo | Muscat |
| 10:25 | 17:25 | 19:25 |

| New Delhi | Hanoi | Beijing |
| 20:55 | 22:25 | 23:25 |

Calculate the following times. Write the times using the 24-hour clock.

The first one is done for you.

When it is 13:25 in Cairo, what time is it in Muscat? → 15:25

1   When it is 07:30 in New Delhi, what time is it in Beijing?

2   When it is 15:45 in Muscat, what time is it in Hanoi?

3   When it is 17:15 in New Delhi, what time is it in Cairo?

4   When it is 09:25 in Hanoi, what time is it in Mexico City?

5   When it is 23:30 in Beijing, what time is it in New Delhi?

6   When it is midnight in New Delhi, what time is it in Cairo?

7   When it is noon in Mexico City, what time is it in Beijing?

Stretch zone

Find out the time difference between your home and Sydney.

Find out the time difference between your home and New York.

When you arrive at school, what time is it in Sydney and in New York?

8C Time zone problems

Explore

Student Book 6, page 145

This timetable shows a list of flight departures from Dubai airport.

Use the list of time differences to help you complete the timetable.

The first one is done for you.

> You need to add the flight duration to the departure time and then add or subtract the time difference.

Time differences compared with Dubai

Sydney, Australia	+ 6 hours	Kuala Lumpur, Malaysia	+ 4 hours
Dhaka, Bangladesh	+ 2 hours	Toronto, Canada	– 8 hours
Tokyo, Japan	+ 5 hours	Anchorage, Alaska	– 12 hours
Nairobi, Kenya	– 1 hour	London, United Kingdom	– 3 hours
Phnom Penh, Cambodia	+ 3 hours		

	Destination	Departure time	Flight duration	Arrival (local time)
	Sydney	09:15	12 hours 30 minutes	03:45 (the next day)
1	Dhaka	10:25	5 hours 15 minutes	
2	Tokyo	10:45	9 hours 10 minutes	
3	Nairobi	13:35	5 hours 25 minutes	
4	Phnom Penh	15:50	6 hours 45 minutes	
5	Kuala Lumpur	19:25	7 hours 15 minutes	
6	Toronto	20:25	15 hours 45 minutes	
7	Anchorage	22:10	17 hours 45 minutes	
8	London	22:15	6 hours 50 minutes	

Stretch zone

I want to be in London for a meeting that starts at 9.00 a.m.

I know the transfer from London airport to the meeting will take 90 minutes.

What time should I aim to leave Dubai?

Review

I Draw a face next to each bubble to show how confident you feel about your learning.

converting between units of time

calculating start and end times and durations

using timetables

solving problems involving different time zones

 2 Tell a partner about one thing you did really well in this unit.

3 Write about what you found easy, what challenged you or what you found really hard.

What work did you feel really confident doing?

_____

_____

_____

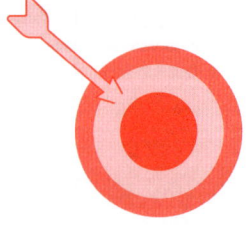

What work really stretched and challenged you?

_____

_____

_____

_____

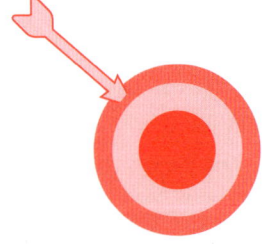

Is there any work you might need some extra help with?

_____

_____

9A Classifying 2D shapes

Discover
Student Book 6, pages 149–150

Follow these steps.

- Fold a sheet of paper. Fold it as many times as you like and at any angle.
- Use a ruler to draw a straight line all the way across the folded paper.
- Cut along the straight line.
- Unfold the pieces.

- sheets of paper
- a ruler
- scissors

Have you made at least four polygons? Are some of them different from each other?

If not, follow the steps again.

How many different polygons did you make with a single cut?

Sketch four of your polygons.

Name each type and write two of its properties.

Sketch of polygon	Type of polygon	Property 1	Property 2

Stretch zone

Is it possible to make all the different types of quadrilateral (square, rectangle, rhombus, parallelogram, trapezium and kite) by making just one cut?

See how many of these shapes you can make.

9A Classifying 2D shapes

Explore
Student Book 6, page 151

Write three properties of each shape.

	Shape	Property 1	Property 2	Property 3
1	scalene triangle			
2	regular heptagon			
3	rhombus			
4	trapezium			
5	isosceles triangle			
6	kite			
7	right-angled triangle			
8	parallelogram			
9	regular hexagon			

Stretch zone

What is the same about a regular and an irregular polygon? What is different?

9B Properties of 2D shapes

Discover   Student Book 6, page 152

Draw polygons with these properties. Each shape must be different.

Write the geometrical name of each shape.

	Properties	Sketch	Name
1	number of sides: 4 base length: 5 cm perpendicular height: 3 cm pairs of opposite sides are parallel.		
2	number of sides: 4 base length: 5 cm perpendicular height: 3 cm pairs of opposite sides are parallel.		
3	number of sides: 4 base length: 5 cm perpendicular height: 3 cm only one pair of opposite sides is parallel.		
4	number of sides: 4 perpendicular height: 3 cm all sides are a different length.		

Stretch zone

Think of a polygon. Write its properties.

Give the list of properties to a partner and ask them to draw the shape.

There should be two different possibilities for the shape.

9B Properties of 2D shapes

Explore 1

Student Book 6, pages 154–155

Draw ten different 2D shapes here.

A	B	C	D	E
F	G	H	I	J

Decide on the criteria for your Carroll diagram.

Sort your shapes by writing the letters in the diagram.

Remember:

each pair of criteria must be opposites, with no overlap.

Here are some examples.

- Is a quadrilateral; Is not a quadrilateral
- Has at least one right angle; Has no right angles
- Has at least one pair of parallel sides; Has no parallel sides

Stretch zone

Sort the same 2D shapes using a Venn diagram. Choose any criteria you like.

9B Properties of 2D shapes

Explore 2
Student Book 6, page 156

1 On the grid, draw a shape or a pattern with order of rotational symmetry 4.

Start by drawing a simple shape. You can then add more detail if you like.

2 On the grid, draw a shape or a pattern with order of rotational symmetry 3.

Stretch zone

Use the Internet to find examples of patterns with rotational symmetry.

Discover

Student Book 6, pages 157–158

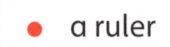
- a ruler

Find six examples of different polyhedra in the environment. Include prisms and pyramids.

Draw the shapes, as accurately as possible.

Name each shape. Write the number of faces, vertices and edges.

> Remember:
>
> a polyhedron (plural: polyhedra) is a 3D shape with flat faces.

Name of shape with sketch or photograph	Number of ...			Name of shape with sketch or photograph	Number of ...		
	faces	vertices	edges		faces	vertices	edges

Stretch zone

Find a 3D shape that you do not know the name of.

Draw it. Then find out the name (for example by searching online).

9C Properties of 3D shapes

Explore Student Book 6, page 159

Write three properties of each shape.

	Shape	Property 1	Property 2	Property 3
1	hemisphere			
2	tetrahedron			
3	dodecahedron			
4	octahedron			
5	triangular prism			
6	square-based pyramid			
7	triangle-based pyramid			

8 Draw a sequence of four 3D shapes. Each shape in the sequence must share a property with the shape before and after it.

Stretch zone

True or false? A hemisphere is not a 3D shape because it has a curved face.

Explain your answer.

9D Making 2D representations of 3D shapes

Discover
Student Book 6, pages 160–162

- three different shaped cardboard boxes
- ruler or tape measure

Open the boxes out so that you can see the nets.

Draw scale drawings of the nets below. Write the scales you used.

Label each drawing with the measurements you took.

scale: _____

scale: _____

scale: _____

Stretch zone

Calculate the volume of each box. Write the volumes next to your drawings.

9D Making 2D representations of 3D shapes

- a selection of boxes

Follow these steps twice.

- Make a model by putting two boxes together.
- Draw your model.
- Draw the plan view, the front elevation and the side elevation.

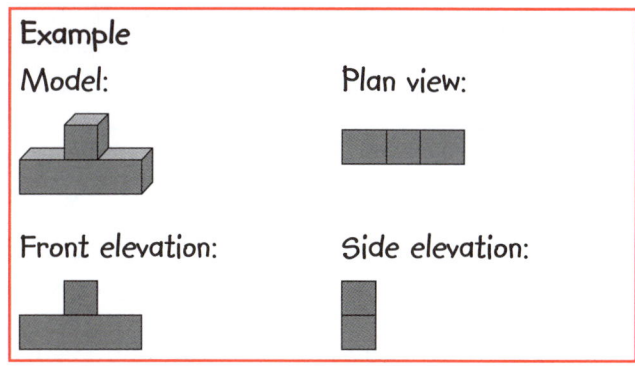

Example
Model: Plan view:

Front elevation: Side elevation:

Model I	Front elevation
Plan	Side elevation
Model 2	Front elevation
Plan	Side elevation

Stretch zone

Write instructions for using the plans to calculate the volume of one of your models.

Discover   Student Book 6, page 165

- ruler
- protractor ('Stretch zone' only)

Draw 12 different triangles by joining dots on the grid.

Include some isosceles, some scalene and some right-angled triangles.

Label the acute angles '**A**', the obtuse angles '**O**' and the right angles '**R**'.

Write the name of each triangle underneath the drawing.

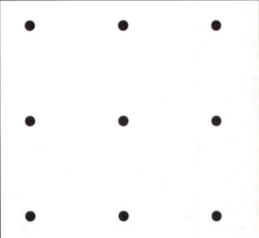 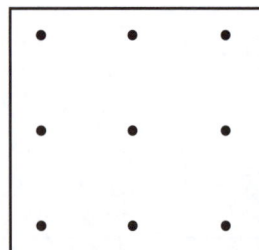 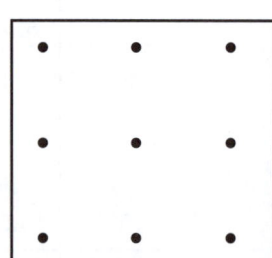 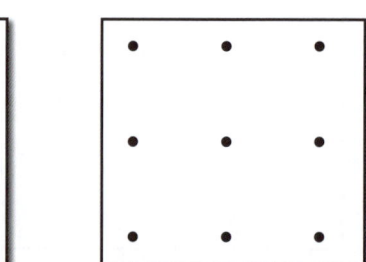

 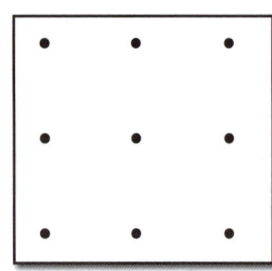 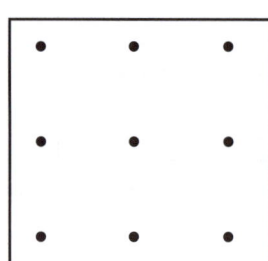 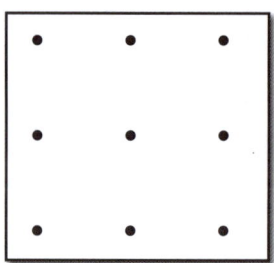

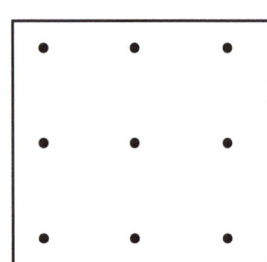 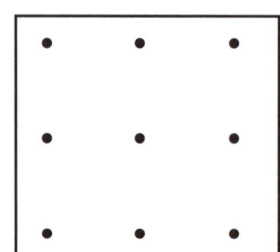 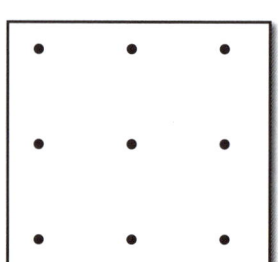

Stretch zone

Choose one of the triangles. Measure each angle and one of the sides.

Use these measurements to draw an exact copy of the triangle.

9E Angles in shapes

Explore   Student Book 6, page 166

- a ruler
- a protractor

When you make a scale drawing, the angles stay the same.

Find four different 2D shapes in your home or classroom.

Measure the sides and the angles. Make a scale drawing of each shape.

Name of shape: _____	Name of shape: _____
Scale: _____	Scale: _____
Name of shape: _____	Name of shape: _____
Scale: _____	Scale: _____

 **Stretch zone**

Find an example of a composite shape. Make a scale drawing of it.

9F Missing angles

Discover

Complete these sentences.

Remember:
the angles in a triangle total 180°.
$a + b + c = 180°$

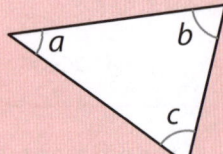

1 Each angle in an equilateral triangle is [ ] °

because _____

_____ .

2 If the two angles at the base of an isosceles triangle are 50°, the other angle is

[ ] ° because _____ .

3 If two angles in a triangle are 50° and 40°, it must be a/an

_____ triangle.

Label the missing angles in these triangles. They are not drawn accurately.

4
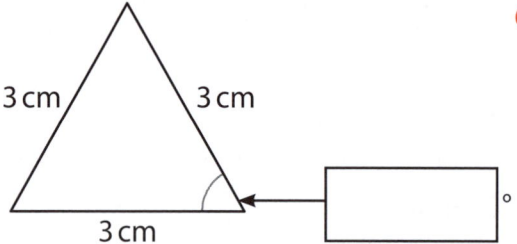
3 cm / 3 cm / 3 cm

6
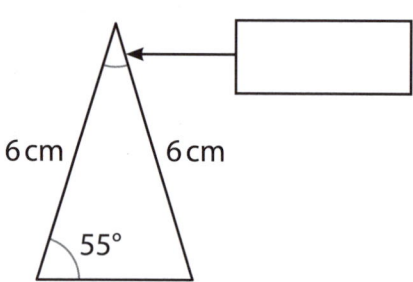
6 cm / 6 cm / 55°

5
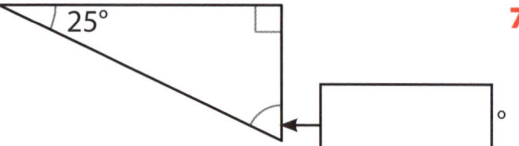
25°

7
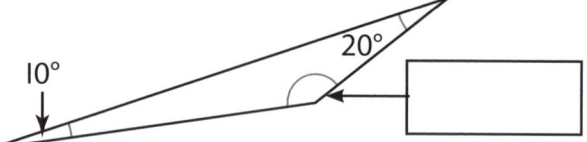
10° / 20°

Stretch zone

You know that the sum of the angles in a quadrilateral is 360°.

How can this help you remember that the sum of the angles in a triangle is 180°?

_____

_____

Explore   Student Book 6, page 168

Find the size of each missing angle.

The diagrams are not drawn accurately.

1

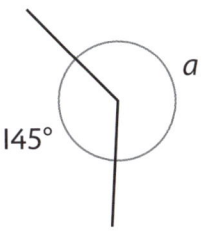

145°   a

a = [   ] °

4

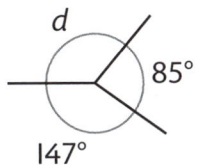

d   85°

147°

d = [   ] °

Remember:

the angles around a point total 360°.

$a + b + c = 360°$

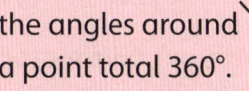

c   a

b

the angles on a straight line total 180°.

$d + e = 180°$

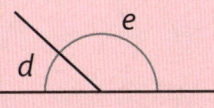

d   e

2

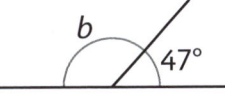

b   47°

b = [   ] °

5

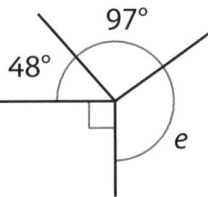

97°

48°

e

e = [   ] °

7

h   32°

h = [   ] °

3

147°

c

c = [   ] °

6

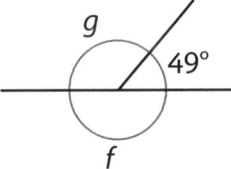

g   49°

f

f = [   ] °

g = [   ] °

8

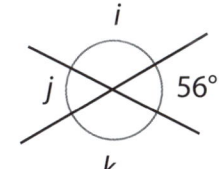

i   56°

j

k

i = [   ] °

j = [   ] °

k = [   ] °

Stretch zone

Use the diagram for **question 8**, and the fact that angles on a straight line add up to 180°, to prove that angles at a point add up to 360°.

Discover · Student Book 6, page 169

Write the correct part of a circle to match each diagram.

radius   diameter   circumference   arc   chord

sector   segment   tangent   centre

1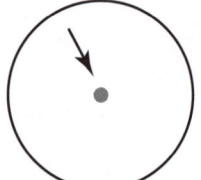

_____

4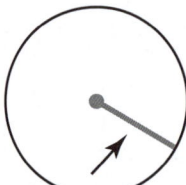

_____

7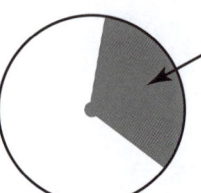

_____

2

_____

5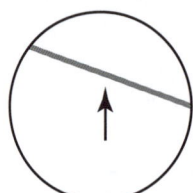

_____

8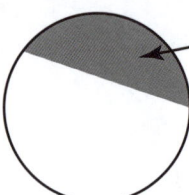

_____

3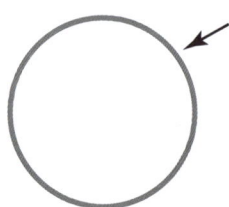

_____

6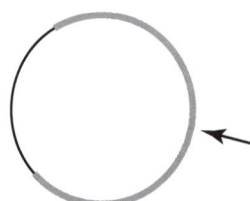

_____

9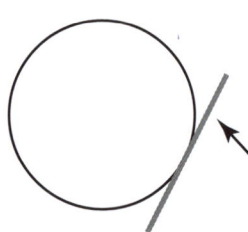

_____

Complete these sentences.

The radius is _____ the length of the diameter.

The diameter is _____ the length of the radius.

 **Stretch zone**

 Choose three of the words above. Write a definition of each one.

9G Circles

Explore   Student Book 6, page 170

- a pair of compasses   • a ruler

I   Draw a circle with radius 3 cm.

Shade a sector.
Draw a radius and an arc.

Label these parts:

- sector

- radius

- arc.

2   Draw a circle with diameter 7 cm.

Shade a segment.
Draw a diameter and a chord.

Label these parts:

- segment

- diameter

- chord.

Stretch zone

Make a pattern of circles. The circles must all have radius 2.5 cm.

9 Geometry – properties of shapes

Review

I Draw a face next to each bubble to show how confident you feel about your learning.

classifying shapes based on their properties

drawing 2D shapes accurately

building 3D shapes and making nets

finding unknown angles

naming the parts of a circle

2 Tell a partner about one thing you did really well in this unit.

3 Write about what you found easy, what challenged you or what you found really hard.

What work did you feel really confident doing?

_____

_____

_____

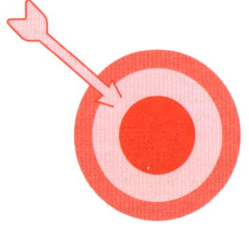

What work really stretched and challenged you?

_____

_____

_____

_____

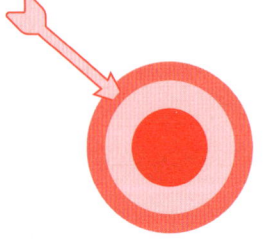

Is there any work you might need some extra help with?

_____

_____

10A Reading and plotting coordinates

Discover

Student Book 6, page 174

Use this coordinate grid to draw a plan of a room in your home.

The origin should be in the centre of the room.

Remember:

the origin (0, 0) is where the two axes cross.

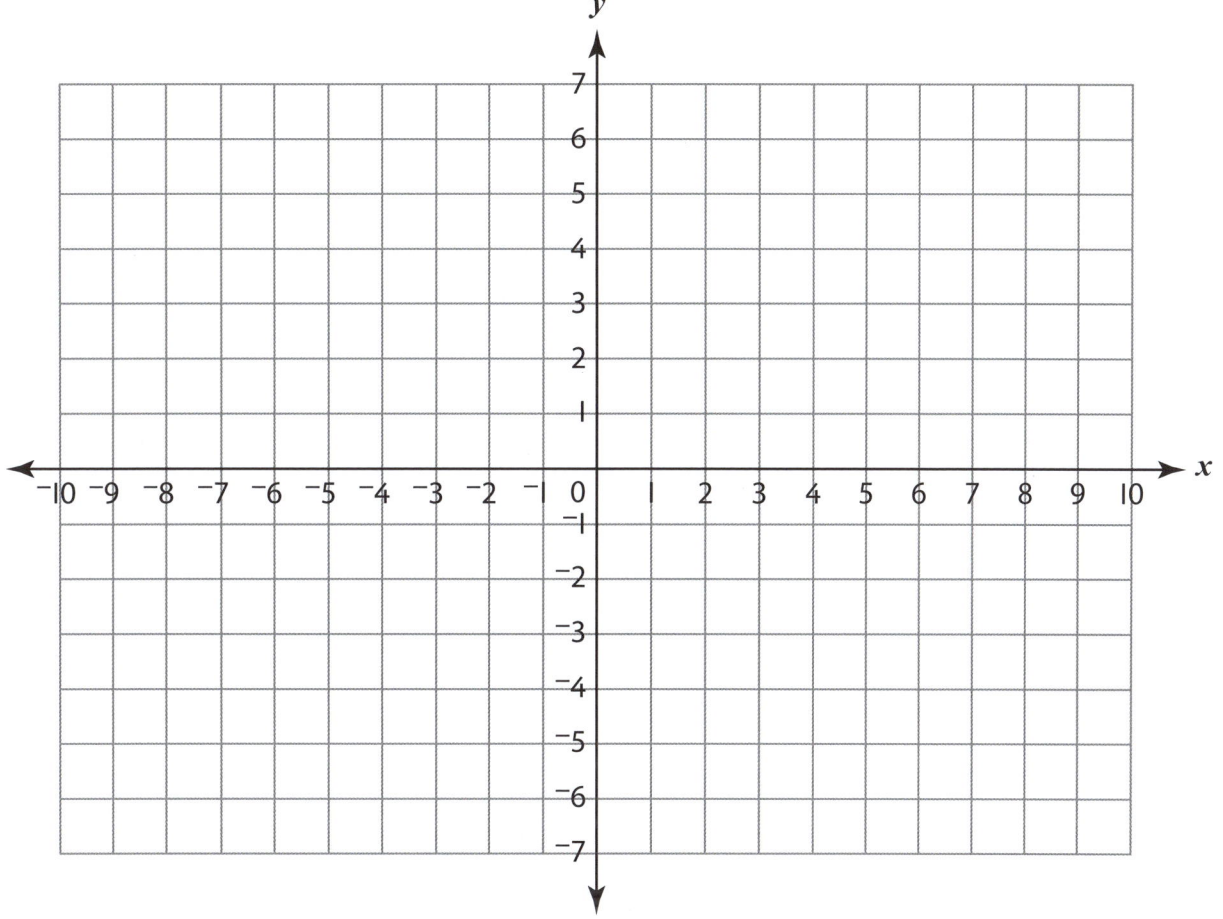

Write the coordinates of four objects in the room.

The coordinates of _____ are (⬚ , ⬚)

The coordinates of _____ are (⬚ , ⬚)

The coordinates of _____ are (⬚ , ⬚)

The coordinates of _____ are (⬚ , ⬚)

Stretch zone

Draw an object on the coordinate grid at these coordinates: (⁻1.5, ⁻4.5)

Explore   Student Book 6, pages 175–176

Draw an irregular hexagon anywhere on this grid.

Label the coordinates of the vertices.

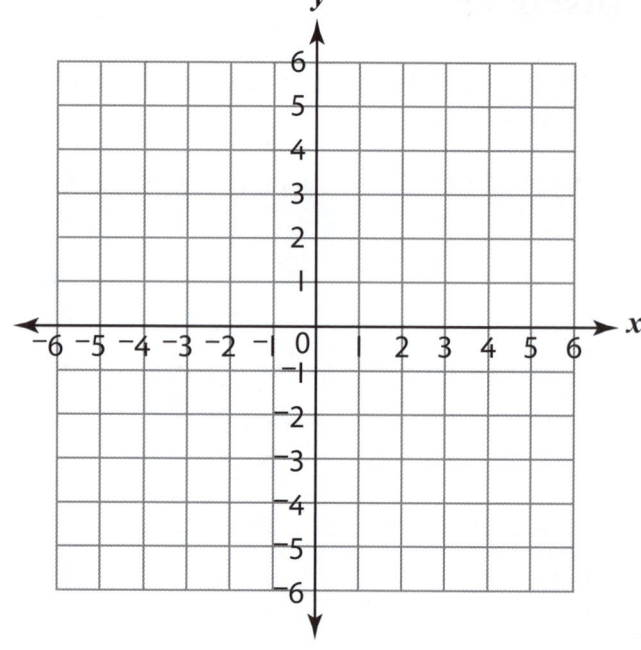

Look at this list of coordinates:

(2, ⁻1) (0,3) (⁻5,1) (⁻5, ⁻5) (⁻2, ⁻1) (⁻5, ⁻2)

Do not plot them yet.

Do you think these could be the vertices of a hexagon?

_____

_____

Now plot the coordinates on this grid.

Can you join them to make a hexagon?

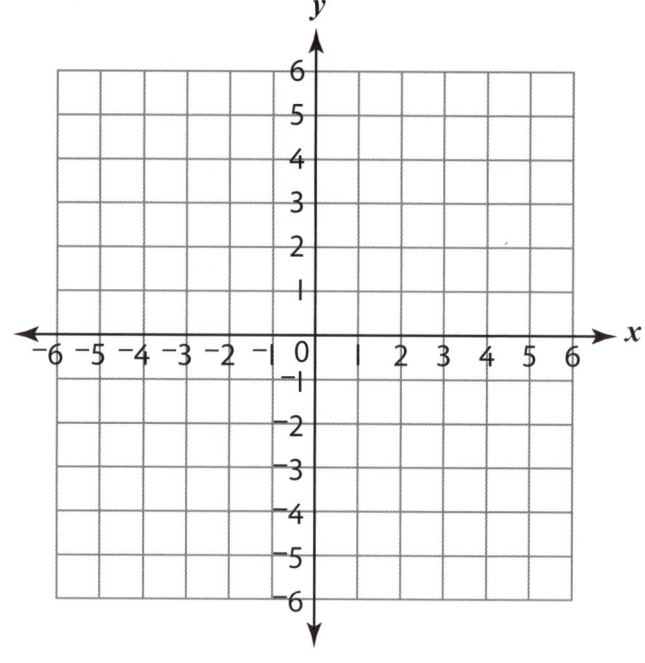

Stretch zone

Draw another hexagon on one of the grids. Try to make it as similar as possible to a regular hexagon. Write the coordinates of the vertices.

_____

10B Translations and reflections

Discover

Student Book 6, page 177

- a ruler
- colouring pencils

You can also include rotational symmetry if you like.

Create a pattern that includes reflections and translations.

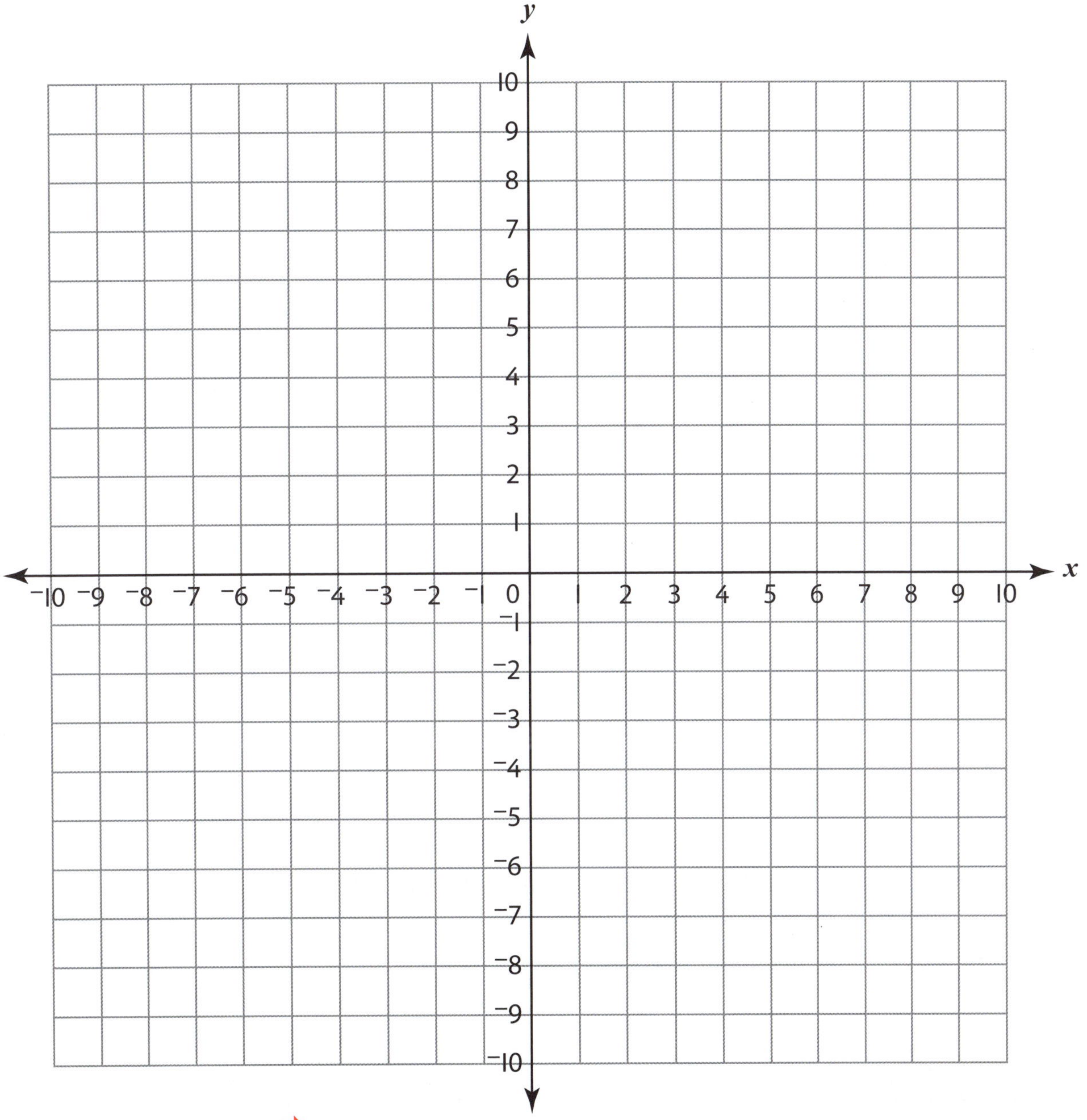

Stretch zone

 Find a pattern in your home that includes translations.

Sketch it as accurately as possible.

Explore   Student Book 6, pages 178–179

Draw a simple shape in the first quadrant on the grid.

One straight edge should be along the x-axis.

Label the coordinates of the vertices.

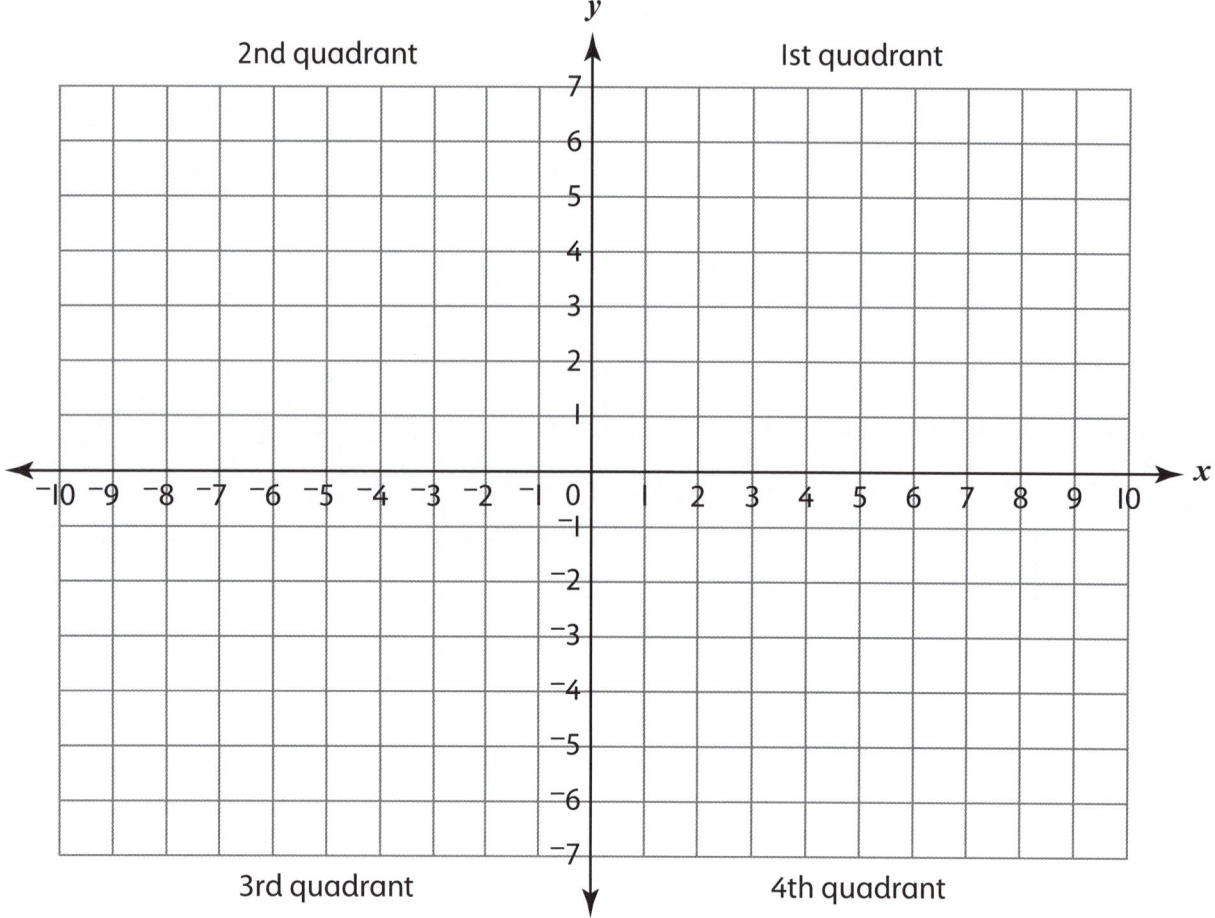

Reflect the shape in the x-axis. Label the coordinates of the new vertices.

Reflect your second shape in the y-axis. Label the coordinates of the new vertices.

Reflect your third shape in the x-axis. Label the coordinates of the new vertices.

Stretch zone

What do you notice about the final reflection and the original shape?

_____

_____

10 Geometry – position and direction

Review

1 Draw a face next to each bubble to show how confident you feel about your learning.

> plotting points on a coordinate grid with four quadrants ◯

> reflecting shapes on a coordinate grid ◯

> translating shapes on a coordinate grid ◯

2 Tell a partner about one thing you did really well in this unit.

3 Write about what you found easy, what challenged you or what you found really hard.

What work did you feel really confident doing?

_____

_____

_____

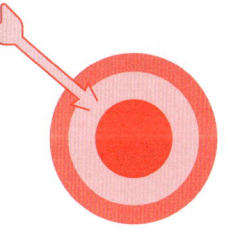

What work really stretched and challenged you?

_____

_____

_____

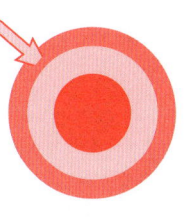

Is there any work you might need some extra help with?

_____

_____

Discover
Student Book 6, page 183

Carry out a survey then find the mean of the data set.
Follow these steps for each question.

• a calculator

- Record your own answer to the question.
- Ask five other people the question and record their answers.
- Calculate the mean of the data set.

1 How much time do you spend using your phone each day?

	You	1	2	3	4	5	Total
Time							

Mean time = _____ ÷ 6 = _____

2 How long does it take you to get to school/work?

	You	1	2	3	4	5	Total
Time							

Mean time = _____ ÷ 6 = _____

3 What is the distance from your home to school/work (to the nearest 100 m)?

	You	1	2	3	4	5	Total
Distance							

Mean distance = _____ ÷ 6 = _____

4 How much time do you spend watching television each night?

	You	1	2	3	4	5	Total
Time							

Mean time = _____ ÷ 6 = _____

Stretch zone

Compare the mean time to get to school/work with the data from the lesson.

Why do you think the results are different?

11A Averages

Explore   Student Book 6, page 184

- a calculator
- a map

Countries with long life expectancy

Country	Hong Kong	Japan	Singapore	Italy	Spain	Switzerland	Australia	Iceland	Israel	South Korea
Life expectancy	84.7	84.5	83.8	83.6	83.4	83.4	83.3	82.9	82.8	82.8

1   What is the mean life expectancy in these countries?

	years

Countries with short life expectancy

Country	Cameroon	Mali	Equatorial Guinea	Guinea-Bissau	South Sudan	Cote d'Ivoire	Nigeria	Sierra Leone	Chad	Lesotho
Life expectancy	58.9	58.9	58.4	58	57.6	57.4	54.3	54.3	54	53.7

2   What is the mean life expectancy in these countries?

	years

3   What is the difference in mean life expectancy in the two sets of countries?

	years

4   Find the countries on a map.

What is the same and what is different about the locations of the countries in each set?

_____

_____

_____

Stretch zone

Research the life expectancy in your own country and five nearby countries. Find the mean.

11B Probability

Discover   Student Book 6, page 185

Explain why each statement is incorrect.

	Statement	This is incorrect because …
1	It is harder to roll a 6 on a dice because that is the number you have to roll to start some board games.	
2	There are about 50% males and females in the world. That means that if a woman already has a girl her next baby will be a boy.	
3	It is the rainy season. That means it is certain that it will rain tomorrow.	
4	If two football teams play each other there is a $\frac{1}{3}$ chance of a home win, an away win or a draw because they are the only three possibilities.	
5	There is a 1 in 10 chance of winning a game. I have lost 9 times in a row. That means I am certain to win the next game.	
6	It is the 100 m final in the Olympics. There are eight runners. That means there is a 1 in 8 chance that any of the runners will win.	

Stretch zone

How can you calculate an approximate probability of a runner winning the Olympic final?

_____

_____

11B Probability

Explore   Student Book 6, pages 186–187

Find the probabilities of these events. Complete the table. One is done for you.

Chosen outcome	Number of equally likely outcomes	Number of possible chosen outcomes	Probability (fraction)
picking a multiple of 3 out of a set of number cards 1–20	20 (There are 20 cards to pick from.)	6 (There are 6 multiples of 3 between 1 and 20.)	$\frac{6}{20} = \frac{3}{10}$
1 rolling an odd number on a 1–6 dice			
2 rolling a total of 9 on two dice			
3 rolling an even number on a 1–10 dice			

Stretch zone

Write down something with a probability of $\frac{1}{3}$.

_____

11C Handling data extended project

Activity 1
Student Book 6, page 188

Write the name of your country (country A) and two other countries.

Country A: _____ Country C: _____

Country B: _____

Use the Internet to find the mean temperature (in °C) on the first day of each month in each country.

Use what you find out to complete the table.

Mean temperature (in °C) on the first day of each month in three countries

Country	1st Jan	1st Feb	1st Mar	1st Apr	1st May	1st Jun	1st Jul	1st Aug	1st Sep	1st Oct	1st Nov	1st Dec
A												
B												
C												

Write four facts about this data.

1 _____

_____

2 _____

_____

3 _____

_____

4 _____

_____

Stretch zone ➡

Write something that surprises you about the data. Explain why you find it surprising.

_____

_____

- colouring pencils: four colours   • a ruler

Draw a comparison line graph to compare your data from page 148.

Include a key to show which colour line represents each country.

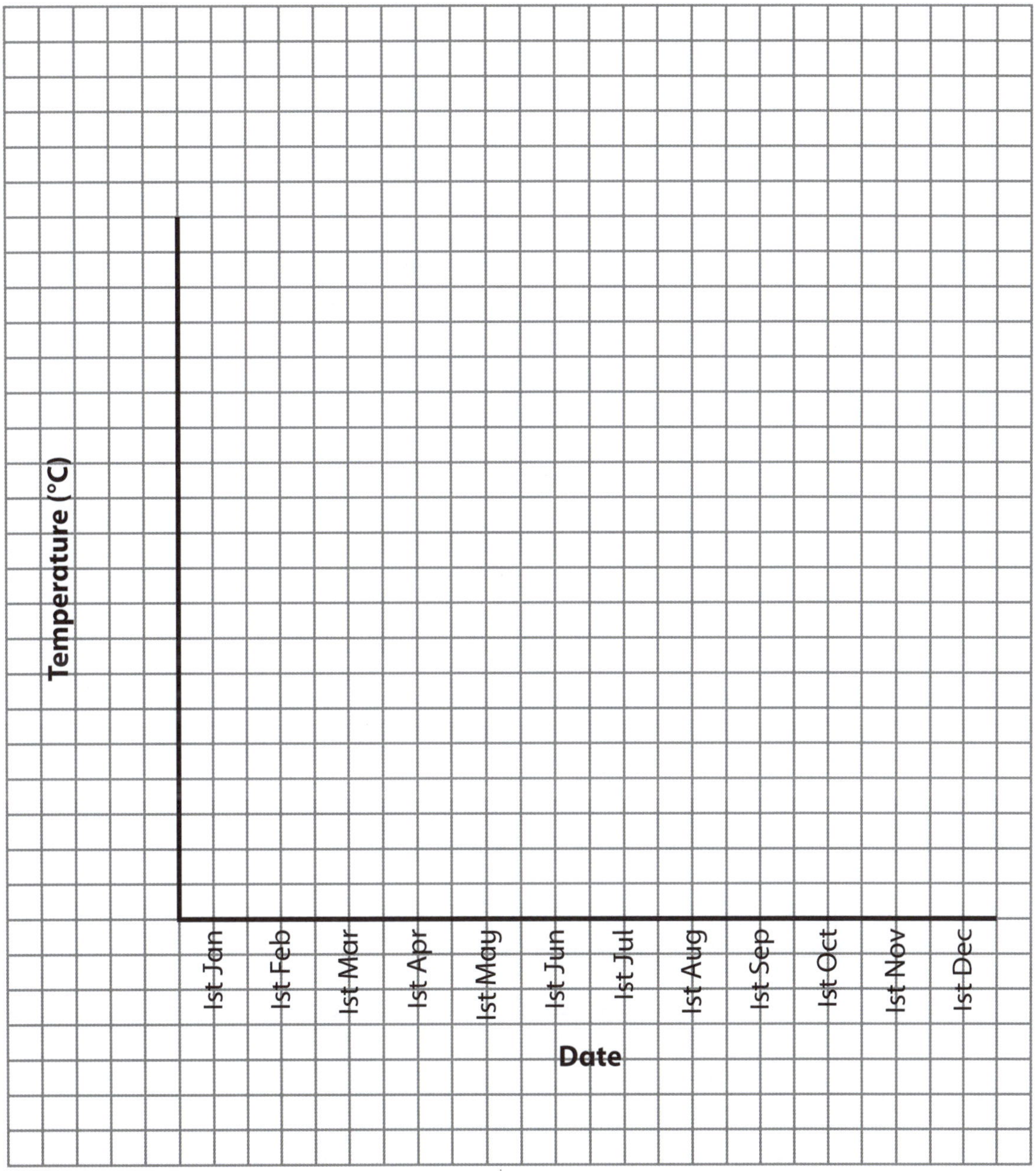

Temperature (°C)

1st Jan 1st Feb 1st Mar 1st Apr 1st May 1st Jun 1st Jul 1st Aug 1st Sep 1st Oct 1st Nov 1st Dec

Date

Stretch zone

Compare your line graph with your table on page 148.

What are the advantages and disadvantages of a line graph and a table?

Activity 3 — Student Book 6, page 190

Think of two questions to ask people. Choose things you are interested in.

Select four answer options for each question.

Collect data from ten people.

Here are some examples of questions you could ask.

What is your favourite genre of book?

What is your favourite food?

What is your favourite thing to do in your spare time?

Question I: _____

_____

Category				
Number of people				

Question 2: _____

_____

Category				
Number of people				

Stretch zone

Repeat the survey with ten different people. Compare the results.

Activity 4   Student Book 6, page 191

Draw pie charts to represent the data in the tables on page I50.

- a protractor
- a ruler

Title: _____

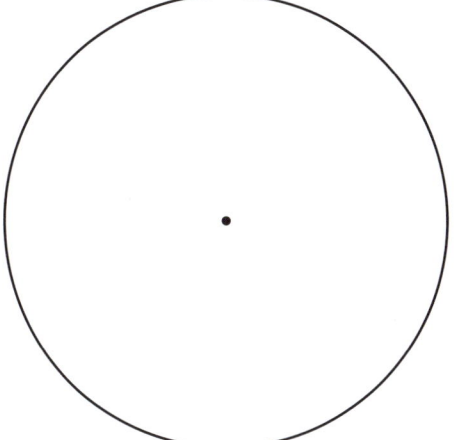

Key

☐ _____

☐ _____

☐ _____

☐ _____

Title: _____

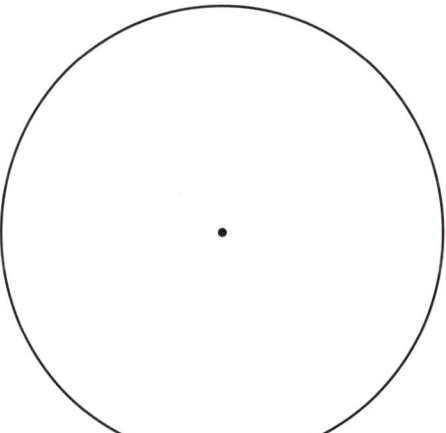

Key

☐ _____

☐ _____

☐ _____

☐ _____

Stretch zone

What is the same and what is different about the two pie charts?

_____

_____

_____

Review

1 Draw a face next to each bubble to show how confident you feel about your learning.

mean average

probability

line graphs

pie charts

collecting, representing and interpreting data

 2 Tell a partner about one thing you did really well in this unit.

3 Write about what you found easy, what challenged you or what you found really hard.

What work did you feel really confident doing?

_____

_____

_____

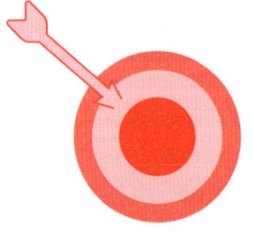

What work really stretched and challenged you?

_____

_____

_____

_____

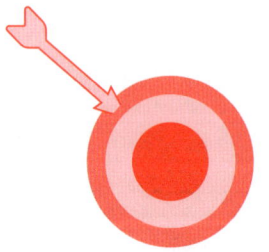

Is there any work you might need some extra help with?

_____

_____